The Book of

LONDON PLACE NAMES

Also by Caroline Taggart:

The Book of English Place Names

The Book of
LONDON PLACE NAMES

CAROLINE TAGGART

EBURY
PRESS

1 3 5 7 9 10 8 6 4 2

First published in 2012 by Ebury Press, an imprint of Ebury Publishing
A Random House Group company

Copyright © Caroline Taggart 2012

Caroline Taggart has asserted her right to be identified as the author of this
Work in accordance with the Copyright, Designs and Patents Act 1988

All map details taken from Bacon's New Map of London, 1902

The Random House Group Limited Reg. No. 954009

Addresses for companies within the Random House Group can be found at
www.randomhouse.co.uk

A CIP catalogue record for this book is available from the British Library

The Random House Group Limited supports The Forest Stewardship Council
(FSC®), the leading international forest certification organisation. Our books
carrying the FSC label are printed on FSC® certified paper. FSC is the only
forest certification scheme endorsed by the leading environmental organisations,
including Greenpeace. Our paper procurement policy can be found at
www.randomhouse.co.uk/environment

Designed and set by seagulls.net

Printed and bound by CPI Group (UK) Ltd, Croydon, CR0 4YY

ISBN 9780091940454

To buy books by your favourite authors and register for offers visit
www.randomhouse.co.uk

For Camille and Mishak, in the hope that they
will one day love London as much as I do

ACKNOWLEDGEMENTS

My heartfelt thanks to Peter, who knows more about London than anyone I know, for putting me right in lots of places. Thanks also to Ryan for telling me about Boudicca and for other less respectable stories; and to Rebecca, Liz, designer Lucy and everyone at Ebury for hard work, support and enthusiasm.

CONTENTS

INTRODUCTION

John Stow, the great Elizabethan chronicler whose work will be much referred to in the following pages, begins his *Survey of London* by quoting the earlier Welsh historian Geoffrey of Monmouth. According to Geoffrey, London was founded in about 1108 BC by Brute or Brutus, a descendant of 'the demi-god Aeneas, the son of Venus, daughter of Jupiter' who was also the ancestor of Romulus and Remus, legendary founders of Rome.

Stow goes on to quote the Roman historian Livy as saying that, when writing of antiquity, it is acceptable to 'interlace divine matters with human, to make the first foundation of cities more honourable, more sacred, and, as it were, of greater majesty'.

This is Stow's characteristically gentle way of telling us that what Geoffrey of Monmouth had written was tripe. Well-intentioned, entertaining tripe, perhaps, but tripe nevertheless.

That said, the early history of London is vague. The first mention of it comes from the Roman historian Tacitus in the second century AD; he tells us that 'Londinium' is 'much frequented by a number of merchants and trading vessels'. It is unlikely to have been a substantial place before the Roman invasions (Julius Caesar in 55 BC and the Emperor Claudius in 43 AD), but it certainly existed, probably as a small settlement on the hills on either side of the WALBROOK – that is, roughly modern CORN-HILL and Ludgate Hill, on which St Paul's stands. Londinium is certainly a Latinised version of an older, British name, and attempts to explain its meaning have occupied scholars for centuries. Geoffrey of Monmouth's story of King Lud (described under Ludgate in the box *The City Gates*, page 37) is generally discounted; other suggestions include 'settlement associated with Londinos', a nickname that might have been given to a man known for his boldness, or 'settlement at the unfordable part of the river'. This last would be geographically accurate – the lowest fordable point was at WESTMINSTER, some 3 kilometres upstream from the original settlement. It seems to be the favoured explanation at the moment, but who knows when further information may come to light and change people's minds?

Also lost in the mists of time is the meaning of London's most significant natural feature, the Thames. It too is of pre-Roman origin and may mean something as simple as 'flowing'. A fairly basic name for a river, you might think, but then it would have been the only major one that the early inhabitants of London knew. Modern-day London-ers still refer to it as 'the river', as if it was the only one that existed or at least the only one that mattered, and this may well have been the rationale for the Celts of 2,000 and more years ago.

Very few Celtic place names have survived in the London area; those that have tend to refer to physical features (rivers, hills, etc.) rather than settlements. The rivers BRENT and the Lea that gives its name to LEYTON and LEYTONSTONE are Celtic in origin, and the otherwise unremarkable suburb of PENGE has, for reasons of its own, also held on to its Celtic roots.

Under Roman rule Londinium grew and prospered. It wasn't a major garrison, but it was an important trading place, with a wall (see LONDON WALL), a forum near the site of today's LEADENHALL Market, an amphitheatre under the Guildhall (see GRESHAM STREET), and all the other trappings of Roman civilisation. In due course, however, the Roman Empire started to collapse and the Roman forces withdrew from Britain. Leaving, as far as London is concerned, almost no surviving place names, but a structure of walls, gates and roads that would define the city, off and on, for another thousand years.

The city at this time was a smaller version of what we now call the City: the wall confined an area rather less than today's 'square mile'. That was to change when the Roman stranglehold on Britain weakened. Three different groups from across the Channel – the Angles, the Saxons and the Jutes – began first to raid the coastline and then from the fifth century to invade and settle. The ones who took over the area round London were the Saxons. They founded what became the mighty kingdom of Wessex (the West Saxons, with their capital at Winchester) but also established southern, eastern and 'middle' groups that are remembered in the names of Sussex, Essex and Middlesex. Their language was what we have come to call Old English and it was more influential in the naming of English settlements than any other before or since.

For some reason the Saxons settled not within the London walls but further west, along what is now the STRAND. Perhaps it was simply that they didn't care for cities in the way that the Romans did: they were more likely to create a number of smaller settlements than the one very large one that the Romans viewed as the focal point of civilised life. That doesn't mean that the Saxons were disorganised – far from it. Bede (673–735), the Northumbrian-based monk regarded as the father of English history, wrote that in the early seventh century London was 'a trading centre for many nations who visit it by land and sea' and late twentieth-century excavations in the region of COVENT GARDEN found evidence of a much more substantial town than had previously been suspected. The Saxon settlement was called Lundenwīc, with the Old English word for a trading place or harbour added to their version of the existing name.

Britain – or England, as this part of it was soon to become – was never peaceful for long in this period; and the next major upheaval was caused by the arrival of the Danes. Invaders from Scandinavia, also known as Vikings or Norsemen, had taken over most of northern England by the end of the 860s and soon turned their attention to the south, where the kingdom of Wessex was the only one to put up serious resistance.

Wessex was lucky to have as its ruler the man we now know as Alfred the Great. He came to the throne in 871, by which time the Danes, after a series of bloody massacres (or so the English chroniclers describe them), had occupied London. In 878 Alfred defeated the Danes in a battle in Wiltshire that was decisive enough for him to do a deal: the Danes would convert to Christianity and retain control of the north and east of England (the boundary was a rough diagonal running from London to Chester), leaving Alfred in charge of the rest. To protect his territory, Alfred set about fortifying or refortifying a network of towns known as *burhs*, which became the –*burys* and –*boroughs* of modern maps. Among his most significant rebuilding was that of London. Lundenwīc, along the Strand, became less important; the focus of city life moved back within the security of the walls and the old Londinium became known as Lundenburh, an indication of its fortified status.

It's impossible to be accurate about population figures at this time but, however many of them there were, the Anglo-Saxons established an enormous number of settlements which grew into villages, towns, cities or, in the case of London, were ultimately subsumed into the growing metropolis. Place names from those days contain recurring features that reflect the concerns of daily life and the reason settlements were founded in the first place. One of the reasons for giving a place a name is to be able to tell it apart from another, similar place; another is to point out a distinguishing feature so that strangers can find it. The most common elements in Anglo-Saxon place names are _–ham_ and _–ton_, meaning respectively a homestead and a farmstead. A simple description like that is fine as long as people stay at home; once they start travelling and trading, they need to be able to tell one farmstead or homestead from another. Enter a third very common Old English element, _–ing_, either as an ending in itself or in combination to form _–ingham_ or _–ington_. _Ing_ has a number of subtle variations in meaning which can be summarised as 'an association with' or expanded to 'belonging to the friends or followers of someone'. Thus London abounds with names such as TOTTENHAM, KENSINGTON and PADDINGTON, which tell us that they were originally settled by men called Totta, Cynesige and Padda, or by their family, followers, descendants or whatever. These men were obviously important enough to have places named after them, but sadly they have for the most part left nothing else for us to remember them by.

Other recurring elements describe physical features: the endings of WEMBLEY and BROMLEY tell us that they were once clearings in woods; most places ending in _–den_ or _–don_ are on hills, though confusingly CROYDON is in a valley. Another potential source of confusion is the all too common _–ham_, which in addition to meaning a homestead

(Old English *hām*) may also mean a piece of land in a bend in a river, or other enclosed piece of land (Old English *hamm*). Because early records are often sparse and spelling erratic, it is not always possible to be certain which derivation applies to any given name. Sometimes, though, the lie of the land gives a clue: that is what enables us to be certain that FULHAM and Twickenham (see the box *The Round Ball and the Oval Ball*, page 240) are *hamms*, but leaves us in doubt about CLAPHAM.

One thing that the Saxons had done before they retreated back inside the City walls was build a church and monastery to the west of Lundenwīc. This may not sound like much – they built churches wherever they went, and no shortage of monasteries either – but this one sowed the seed that made London the 'twin city' it is today. It was on this site that the pious Edward the Confessor (1042–66), the last Saxon king of England, decided not only to expand and rebuild the monastery but also to create a palace. The word 'monastery' is closely related to 'minster', a minster church being one where the monks generally lived apart from the world but 'ministered' to the sick and to any passers-by who needed their hospitality. Edward's project, being to the west of the City, became WESTMINSTER.

You may have noticed in the last paragraph that Edward the Confessor died in 1066, and you don't have to be too hot on English history to recognise that date. It was, in fact, a hectic year. Edward died on 5 January. Harold, Earl of Wessex, claimed the throne and was crowned – at the newly completed Westminster Abbey and with what some would call indecent haste – on 6 January. Other aspirants to the throne promptly rolled up their sleeves and one, Harald Hardrada of Norway, invaded from the north. Harold defeated him at the Battle of

Stamford Bridge, near York, on 25 September, then almost immediately received word that William of Normandy was invading from the south. Harold dashed off to Sussex and, understandably exhausted, was defeated and killed at the Battle of Hastings on 14 October. William marched across southern England to London, burning and pillaging as he went, and settled into the palace at Westminster. He then laid siege to the City. Although he failed to breach the wall's defences, he was scary enough that the City fathers surrendered to him and allowed him to be crowned at Westminster Abbey on Christmas Day. On New Year's Eve the Anglo-Saxons were doubtless raising a surreptitious glass and saying, 'Thank God that's over – roll on 1067.' William became King William I, 'William the Conqueror', and the Norman Conquest had taken its first decisive steps.

The Normans now became the ruling class and Norman French the language of the elite. Its effect on place names is similarly elitist: Norman landowners tended to tack their own names on to existing Old English ones to produce the likes of TOOTING Bec. Anywhere beginning with *Bel–* or *Beau–*, such as BELSIZE PARK, is likely to come from the French for 'beautiful': they were the only ones who had leisure to admire the scenery. They were also the ones most likely to have time and money to go hunting – see SOHO and ENFIELD Chase.

William didn't carry out his threat to destroy London. He granted its citizens a charter guaranteeing them rights that they had enjoyed in the previous reign and that were by no means all honoured in the rest of the country. The document is written in English and contains the word 'London', spelt as we would spell it today: this isn't the first occasion when Alfred the Great's *–burg* was dropped, but it seems to make it official. London therefore had William's blessing to expand, trade and grow rich. He wasn't taking too many chances, though: he built the White Tower (which remains the central keep of the Tower of London) and a couple of other fortresses to make sure these privileged citizens didn't take any liberties. The Tower also became a royal residence and remained so until Tudor times, though the royal household spent most of its time at the Palace of WESTMINSTER until it moved to WHITEHALL in the sixteenth century and ST JAMES'S in the seventeenth.

It's difficult to say when precisely London became the capital of England. From about the second century AD it had been the most important city in Roman Britain, superseding Colchester – we know from archaeological finds that a lot of trading ships went up and down the river at this time. It was also treated as the capital by some of the Saxon kings. But William and his son William II (1087–1100) continued to carry out some of their affairs of state in Winchester. Transferring the Exchequer from Winchester to London in the twelfth century seems to have been one of the key incidents that tipped the balance in London's favour.

Many City place names reflect the way London expanded during the period following 1066: they refer to markets and business of one sort or another. CHEAPSIDE was the centre of the market area but all the dealers in meat and fish, bread and milk, shoes and stockings tended to congregate in the same place and have the relevant street named after them (see the box *What You See Is What You Get*, page 45). Banking, too, came into its own, in OLD JEWRY and LOMBARD STREET, to name but two.

With prosperity inevitably came population growth: in 1100 London's population was about 25,000, by 1300 this figure had doubled and in 1350 it had not gone down, despite the fact that the Black Death of the 1340s is estimated to have killed about half the City's inhabitants. Spreading outside the walls was an obvious step.

One place to live and work was around the Palace of Westminster, where there was always a need for service industries and the chance of a decent tip. Another was the courts, which grew up between the City and Westminster in the thirteenth century (see the box *In the Name of the Law*, page 139). Places such as FARRINGDON and the BARBICAN, only just outside the walls (indeed, in the case of Farringdon, part inside and part out), expanded, as did the area south of the river that had been part of Alfred the Great's plan to control access to London Bridge – SOUTHWARK.

Skipping forward in time, TV dramas and documentaries have given most of us a rough working knowledge of the Tudor period, but in the context of place names a brief mention of the Dissolution of the Monasteries may not go amiss. In the 1530s, as a direct result of his desire to divorce Catherine of Aragon and marry Anne Boleyn, Henry VIII also became 'divorced' from the Pope. (Nowadays he'd be all over the Sunday papers; in the sixteenth century he was excommunicated. Times change.) Henry now proclaimed himself head of the Church of England. Catholic monasteries, which owed their allegiance to the Pope, were suddenly a threat. 'Dissolving' them not only brought ecclesiastical power back into Henry's hands, it enabled him to confiscate their vast wealth. He could thus both swell his own coffers and give generous pay-outs to his supporters to keep them on side. Names associated with monasteries linger on, however, in BLACKFRIARS, ST JAMES'S and elsewhere.

Elizabeth I, the last of the Tudors, died childless in 1603 and was succeeded by James Stuart, the son of Mary, Queen of Scots. The Stuarts had ruled Scotland for over 200 years and James was already James VI there; he now became James I of England.

One history of Scotland describes the Stuarts as 'a royal family so dreadful that the Scots were even prepared to share them with the English' and that sentence more or less sums them up. Their big problem was that they believed in the Divine Right of Kings. They were kings because God said so, and anything that they said or did was the will of God; they were not answerable to the people, to Parliament or to anyone else on this side of the grave. Across the Channel in France Louis XIV believed much the same thing and got away with it; the problem with the early Stuarts was that they didn't have the political acumen to carry it off. James I's reign (1603–25) was dominated by favouritism, a blatant disregard for Parliament, chronic extravagance and financial mismanagement.

His son Charles I (1625–49) had all his father's weaknesses, in spades. Battles with Parliament over both religion and money were a constant feature of his reign and got so out of hand that the country dissolved into civil war.

It's worth emphasising just how important the religious conflict was. This is barely a century on from the creation of the Church of England. The reigns of James I and Charles I saw the new Church moving, some said, away from its simple, scripture-based roots and back towards the rituals associated with Catholicism. And you have to remember that people cared passionately about this. Or at least the rich and powerful did: the vast majority of the people were probably more concerned with where their next meal was coming from, but senior churchmen had been burnt at the stake over this issue. The Protestant hatred of anything connected with Rome and the Pope was exacerbated by the fact that Charles, although nominally a Protestant, was married to a Catholic French princess, Henrietta Maria, and there were concerns that he would be cajoled into making concessions to the English Catholics. The fact that Charles seems to have made one promise to the French Catholic royals and another to powerful Protestants at home could only add fuel to the fire.

All this led to a very divided country, and specifically to the rise of a sect called Puritanism. The Puritans were dissidents within the Church of England who – in addition to wanting to abolish anything they considered idolatrous or unscriptural, such as ornaments or musical instruments in church – objected to the Church owing allegiance to the King rather than directly to God. Go back a couple of paragraphs to the bit about the Divine Right of Kings and you'll see that there is potential for serious conflict here.

Anyway, back to the Civil War. The combatants were the Royalists (Cavaliers) and the Parliamentarians (Roundheads), latterly led by a Puritan called Oliver Cromwell; incredibly, the war, which tore families apart as well as dividing the country down factional lines, lasted almost seven years. Charles I was eventually defeated, tried for treason and beheaded in WHITEHALL in 1649. His son, also Charles, went into exile. Cromwell took control as Lord Protector and ruled what is known as the Commonwealth of England (and later of Scotland and Ireland too) until his death in 1658. He was succeeded by his son Richard, who didn't have the backing of the military – nor, one suspects, his father's forceful personality – and lasted less than a year. The army ousted him and recalled Charles II, as he was now acknowledged to be, to take the throne. This act and the period that followed it are known as the Restoration.

Puritanism has come to be associated with the suppression of anything that looks like fun. This is not entirely fair, but the received wisdom is that England under Cromwell was a pretty miserable place to be: theatres and pubs were closed, many sports were banned and you could be fined for swearing or put in the stocks for doing unnecessary work on a Sunday. Small wonder then that when Charles II returned and allowed people to enjoy themselves again, they christened him 'the Merry Monarch'.

To revert to the subject of place names – in case you thought we were wandering completely off the track – Charles was understandably grateful to those who had stood by him during his time in exile and rewarded them lavishly. Much of ST JAMES'S and MAYFAIR was developed during and immediately after his reign, because he gave great chunks of real estate to friends and hangers-on. They in turn either parcelled out the land and made money from it or built themselves grand houses; Burlington House, which now houses the Royal Academy, is one example (see BURLINGTON ARCADE). As a result, many streets in this part of town are named after Charles II's chums, their wives, children and people to whom they owed favours.

This continues to be true if you move forward a few decades in time and north a few minutes' walk. The Grosvenor Estate south of OXFORD STREET, the Portland Estate north of it, and to the east land owned by the Dukes of Bedford – all of which had been open fields and farmland – became MAYFAIR, MARYLEBONE, FITZROVIA and BLOOMSBURY. The developments were carefully planned and laid out around elegant squares that survive to this day; the squares and the streets are almost all named after the estate owner, his various titles, members of his family and his properties elsewhere. The street maps of these districts give us example upon example of overwhelming egos and filthy riches on the one hand and shameless sycophancy on the other.

Once you start talking about street names, it is worth noting that they change more than settlement names. Settlement names, witness all those farmsteads and woodland clearings mentioned earlier, tend to hang around long after they have ceased to be accurate. One obvious reason for the changes in street names is that streets are knocked down and replaced: the playwright Ben Jonson was born in 1572 in Hartshorn Alley, which later disappeared under building works round CHARING CROSS; in the 1880s various streets in Soho were destroyed to make way for SHAFTESBURY AVENUE. Others change for the reasons discussed in the box *Changing Names* on page 211. Sadly, there is no mention in the modern *A–Z* of Pickle Herring Stairs, though it was there in 1872, and Strype's Pease Porridge Alley has gone too.

Charles II, despite a slew of mistresses and bastard children, left no legitimate offspring, so his brother succeeded him as James II. Charles had shrewdly juggled the interests of Catholics and Protestants; James had no such ability. He was a committed and public Catholic, and it took only three years for Parliament to decide he was not what they wanted. James was deposed and his Protestant daughter Mary invited, with her equally Protestant husband William of Orange, to rule in his stead. This was in 1688–9; ever since then the British monarch has been forbidden from being or from marrying a Catholic. In the late twentieth century minor royals were still officially giving up their standing as twenty-somethingth in line for the throne because they chose to marry Catholics; as I write this in 2011 it seems likely that this age-old piece of prejudice is finally going to be revoked – but it has been a long time coming.

William and Mary were succeeded by her sister Anne, who also died childless (though not for want of trying – see HANOVER SQUARE). The nearest heir, when you had ruled out about fifty Catholics who had stronger genealogical claims, was a German second cousin who became George I and ushered in the Georgian period also referred to under HANOVER SQUARE. For our purposes – though not for the purposes of the Scots who continued to try to restore James II's descendants – things calmed down.

While all this was going on, London continued to expand. The population in 1650 is estimated at 350,000; in 1700 at 500,000, despite the fact that the Great Plague of 1665 had killed perhaps 100,000 Londoners. By 1801 (the first census) it was close to a million; in 1851 over two million. And they all had to live somewhere.

Technology came into its own here, in three major ways. Substantial parts of the outskirts of London had once been marshes and moors; draining them enabled more people to live in, for example, HACKNEY, LAMBETH and WANDSWORTH. Building the great embankments along the Thames (see VICTORIA EMBANKMENT and MILLBANK) provided road access to such outlying suburbs as CHELSEA, which expanded rapidly in the nineteenth century. And the advent of the railways meant that people working in the City could live as far afield as CLAPHAM, PUTNEY and beyond. All those outlying hamlets, the BALHAMs and the PADDINGTONs, the ISLINGTONs and the STEPNEYs, became part of the same vast built-up area.

This sort of population explosion brought its problems, of course, notably in the slums made famous in the cartoons of William Hogarth (1697–1764) and the novels of Charles Dickens (1812–70). The most notorious, the area round ST GILES, was once perfectly salubrious; then it became too popular and not exclusive enough for the upper classes who had first moved here, away from the crowded City. Those who could afford to moved further west, the price of property in St Giles plummeted and the poor surged in, six or eight to a room. The nineteenth-century authorities managed to ignore quite a lot of this – that's why philanthropists such as Angela Burdett-Coutts (see COLUMBIA ROAD) and campaigning writers such as Dickens were so numerous and so important – but they did get wise to two things. One, they needed to bury these people when they died (see KENSAL GREEN) and two, they needed to provide them with fresh air and open spaces (see FINSBURY/HIGHBURY and ALEXANDRA PALACE). Interesting that the idea for the cemeteries should have come along forty-plus years before the idea for the parks, but that's the way it was.

Queen Victoria's reign (1837–1901) also saw the zenith of one other recurring characteristic of London place names: royalness. At one point it seemed as if every new feature that wasn't called Victoria was called Albert after her husband (and see LANCASTER GATE for an idea of just how desperate this could get). But this was far from being a nineteenth-century phenomenon. There are Charles Streets, James's Streets and George Streets, King Streets and Queens Roads all over the place. The most famous of them are dealt with in the box *Which King, Which Queen?* on page 155 and in individual entries, but clearly 'You can't go wrong sucking up to the royal family' is an attitude that prevailed for some 300 years.

So we come close to the modern age and the modern city, which from the late nineteenth century acquired a more clearly defined administrative structure than it had ever had before. The City of London Corporation has been in existence since time immemorial, but its jurisdiction has only ever extended over the City itself. Until the London County Council (LCC) was created in 1889, local government of other areas was in the hands of metropolitan boroughs or counties: BARKING was in Essex, for example, and EALING in Middlesex. The LCC became responsible for all of what is now Inner London – the first time this area had had a single governing body. It was abolished in 1965 in the course of a major restructuring which created the Greater London Council (GLC, abolished in 1986) and the thirty-two boroughs that today make up Inner and Outer London. One of the new boroughs, surprisingly, was the City of WESTMINSTER: the term has been in use for 500 years, but became official only in 1900 when the Metropolitan Borough of Westminster was granted – by royal charter – the right to call itself a city. Westminster expanded to include the areas round MARYLEBONE and PADDINGTON only in the 1965 reshuffle.

The vast majority of the new boroughs, from HOUNSLOW to HAVERING, adopted existing names, most of them dating back to Anglo-Saxon times. If it ain't broke, don't fix it, may have been the policy; or it may have been motivated by prudence: the entry for FINS-BURY/HIGHBURY shows how fiercely Londoners can react to anyone messing about with their names.

This book is divided into sections that broadly reflect the existing boroughs, with further subdivisions within the Cities of London and Westminster. I have split Westminster into three parts, south, central and north, with KNIGHTSBRIDGE and THE MALL marking the approximate boundary between south and central, and OXFORD STREET separating central from north. Within these three sections there are further subdivisions, some of which are necessarily arbitrary: most people would agree, for example, that SOHO is bounded by CHARING CROSS ROAD, OXFORD STREET, REGENT STREET and SHAFTESBURY AVENUE, but would be less sure about where Victoria ended and BELGRAVIA began.

In addition to individual entries there are boxes scattered through the book covering themes such as railway stations and places named after royalty. Some entries also cover more than one place because the etymology or history of these places is closely connected. Thus Cannon Street and Liverpool Street, King's Road and Queensway do not have entries of their own, Bedford Square is covered under RUSSELL SQUARE, Savile Row gets a passing mention under BURLING-TON ARCADE and so on. All these 'subsidiary' entries are listed in the index, so please check there if it looks as if your favourite place has been left out. Most of the entries are to do with streets or localities. I also thought that a few buildings, such as Big Ben, the Festival Hall and the Ritz Hotel, were worth a mention: they are indicated in the text like so ▓▓.

The place names of London bear witness to a long and complex history. Arrive at PADDINGTON and you are in a place named after a long-forgotten Saxon; come to MARYLEBONE and you are commemorating a church that no longer exists by a stream that is now largely underground; use LONDON BRIDGE and you are at the place where a drawbridge was once raised to stop anyone getting into the City after nine o'clock at night. Wandering the streets in the City you find evidence of ancient markets in amongst the twenty-first-century bankers (and seventeenth-century churches peeping out between later concrete monstrosities); at Waterloo or TRAFALGAR SQUARE or even MAIDA VALE the names evoke victory in long-ago battles; above the shops and the small hotels at street level in MAYFAIR and BLOOMSBURY are the homes that developers once sold to a socially ambitious clientele. Go out into the suburbs – even if it is no further than BALHAM or ACTON – and the names remind you that these were once tiny hamlets far too far from London for anyone to go there on a regular basis.

The only things you need in order to enjoy London to the full are an enquiring mind and a pair of comfortable shoes. Do go and look: it is all there, lurking just below the surface, in the place names.

SOURCES REFERRED TO IN THE TEXT

The Domesday Book (1086) is a remarkable survey, carried out for tax purposes under the auspices of William the Conqueror, to show who owned what land and how much it was worth. It records some 13,000 place names across England and in many cases is the first written mention of them.

Geoffrey of Monmouth (died 1155) wrote a *History of the Kings of Britain* which is our principal source for stories about King Arthur, 'Old King Cole' and Shakespeare's Lear. He is now generally considered to have been an entertaining writer rather than a rigorous historian.

John Stow (c. 1525–1605): London is fortunate to have had a number of antiquarians who made it their life's work to chronicle every possible detail of city life. Stow's *Survey of London*, published in 1598, is a minute account of the roads, buildings, history and people of the city of his day and of several centuries previously. As the introduction to a 1908 edition of the book says, he was blessed with 'a long life, a retentive memory, a zeal for accumulating material, and the painstaking capacity for giving it shape'. Many experts maintain that the *Survey* has never been bettered.

William Camden (1551–1623) compiled the first topographical survey of the British Isles, *Britannia*, published in 1586. He was a friend of Stow and a fellow antiquarian; like Stow he winkled into the origins of place names and was not above reproducing old wives' tales – he may have poo-poohed them, but he wanted to record local folk wisdom as well as what he felt was the truth. Again like Stow, this makes him a surprisingly entertaining read.

John Strype (1643–1737) took Stow's work and expanded on it vastly, to cover the changes that had taken place in the intervening 100-plus years. Not only had London expanded – this is the period when MAYFAIR and WESTMINSTER were becoming built up – but the Great Fire of 1666 had destroyed swathes of the old City, rendering chunks of Stow's work obsolete. Although he is hot on such social issues as public health and water supplies, Strype seems to have been a terrible snob and much concerned with the 'quality' of the people who inhabited the streets he describes.

John Evelyn (1620–1706) and **Samuel Pepys** (1633–1703) were two of the great diarists of their or any other time. Pepys' background was humbler than Evelyn's, but both served at court and became very well connected. From them we glean extraordinary insights into seventeenth-century life.

Daniel Lysons (1762–1834) wrote a four-volume study of *The Environs of London* in the 1790s. His coverage extended about 18 kilometres from the centre of the city, much further than Stow or Strype.

H B Wheatley's three-volume *London Past and Present*, published in 1891, has as a subtitle 'Its history, associations, and traditions'. It contains lots of information on the development of districts and streets, but also a pleasing amount of gossip about who lived there when and how they behaved themselves. Wheatley quotes Pepys, Evelyn and many other early diarists and commentators, giving his work an eminently readable 'I was there' feel.

Ben Weinreb and **Christopher Hibbert's** *London Encyclopaedia*, published in 1983 but recently revised and reissued, expresses a debt to Wheatley and brings the subject matter up to date. Full marks to whoever thought of including buildings and streets that aren't there any more but indicating them with a different typeface.

THE CITY

For many centuries the City of London was enclosed by first the Roman and later the medieval wall (see LONDON WALL). As time went by, however, it expanded and overflowed, so that today 'the square mile' (actually 1.12 square miles, or 290 hectares) spreads west up FLEET STREET, north to the BARBICAN and beyond, and east to encompass LIVERPOOL STREET and the area around (but not including) the Tower. In terms of local government, the City isn't a London borough – it is a separate entity under the jurisdiction of the City of London Corporation, an authority that has been in existence for over 1,000 years. It is also, of course, one of the world's leading financial centres: 'the City', written with a capital C and without further explanation, is universally recognised as meaning 'the City of London' and the financial institutions within it.

WITHIN THE WALL

Even though very little of the wall remains, it is the obvious way to divide the City into two. Most of the entries in this section refer, therefore, to the older part, recalling a time when this was primarily a residential area, needing markets and shops and tradespeople; and recording its rise as a centre for world trade.

———

Aldermanbury

–bury (the source of the modern word *borough*) comes from the Old English for a fortified place, but was later used to describe a manor, the estate of a landowner of substance. It will crop up again and again throughout this book, from CANONBURY to BLOOMSBURY to GUNNERSBURY. In medieval London, an alderman was the chief officer of a ward, next in rank to the mayor. (As a ward is defined as 'a district under the jurisdiction of an alderman', we could go round in circles a bit here, but you get the gist.) Anyway, aldermen could become very wealthy and a number of them lived on a grand scale, comparable to that of the nobility and the highest ranking churchmen, in houses in and near this street. The name is recorded in the twelfth century.

Bank

The underground station sits in the shadow of the Bank of England, established as a concept under William III (1689–1702) and moved to its present building in 1734. Whatever you may read in the papers about the current banking system, the Bank of England is the only institution in the country that really does have a licence to print money. See also THREADNEEDLE STREET.

Bevis Marks

One of the most intriguing names in a city full of intriguing names, this was once called Burie's Markes, because it marked the boundary of land belonging to the Abbots of Bury St Edmunds in Suffolk. This was presumably around the time that St Edmund was performing his miracles at Cripplegate (see the box *The City Gates*, page 37). There has been a synagogue here since the early eighteenth century, but the

Christian connection persists – obscurely enough for most people not to notice – in the name of the street.

Today's synagogue is the oldest in London: when the Jews, expelled by Edward I 400 years earlier, were admitted back into England by Oliver Cromwell (see CHANCERY LANE) they established a congregation just round the corner but moved here when they outgrew their original premises.

Billingsgate

The medieval city was a highly regulated place, and only certain quays on the river were licensed to handle foreign trade. The Steelyard mentioned under DOWGATE HILL was one of them; Queenhithe, which means 'queen's landing place', was another. The queen after whom Queenhithe is named was Matilda, wife of Henry I (1100–35), but subsequent queens retained the right to exact tolls from the goods shipped in and out. Best known of all the quays, perhaps, is Billingsgate, once famous for fish and bad language. The name means 'gate associated with a man named Billing'. Geoffrey of Monmouth, bless him, links it to an ancient king of the Britons called Belinus and, according to Stow, says that 'when he was dead, his body being burnt, the ashes in a vessel of brass were set upon a high pinnacle of stone over the same gate'. There is no evidence for this whatsoever, but it makes a good story.

Blackfriars

The thirteenth century saw wave upon wave of friars of different orders arriving in England, to preach and to care for the poor and the ill (see the box *The Friars* on page 25). Starting their work in the most deprived areas of the City, they soon attracted the admiration of wealthy patrons. Among them were the Black Friars (so called from the colour of their habits) or Dominicans (because they were followers of St Dominic), who had a substantial monastery on the site where Blackfriars Station now stands. No nonsense about poverty for this order: their monastery was large and luxurious enough for the king to use it to accommodate foreign visitors, and for Parliament sometimes to meet in its Great Hall. In fact, so powerful were the Black Friars that they received royal permission to knock down a bit of the ancient City wall and rebuild it to suit their own purposes.

Like so many monasteries throughout the country, this one did not survive the fell hand of Henry VIII. It was 'dissolved' in 1538 and its many buildings sold off. Some of them were used as rehearsal rooms for the boy choristers who also sometimes played women's parts in plays; in 1609 a playhouse, known as the Blackfriars Theatre, appeared on the site and remained – in various incarnations – until it was closed down by the Puritans in the 1640s and demolished in 1655. Shakespeare was at one time a part-owner and, because the playhouse was covered over, his works could be performed here during the winter when the open-air Globe was closed.

Today the monastery is remembered not only in the name of the area but in the gloriously over-the-top art deco pub the Black Friar, tucked into a corner off New Bridge Street. The pub's decor, much of it in marble, depicts the friars going about their daily lives – eating, drinking, singing and fishing – and a plaque on the wall outside explains that the building's unusual shape 'is due to the fact that all the surrounding buildings have long since been demolished, taking with them the small alleyways that were once the only access'.

THE FRIARS

The Black Friars of BLACKFRIARS are not the only religious order to be commemorated in City place names.

The order of the **Grey Friars** or Franciscans (followers of St Francis of Assisi, distinguished by their grey habits) had been founded on the repudiation of all property. Well, that didn't last long. They began their mission in London in a small house in the aptly named Stinking Lane, near Newgate, a street dominated by butchers' shops (it's now King Edward Street, see the box *Changing Names* on page 211) Thanks to the generosity of the local worthies, they were soon able to build themselves a substantial priory. A Wren church, known as Christ Church Greyfriars or Christ Church Newgate Street, built on the site of the Franciscans' chancel, was gutted during the Blitz and never rebuilt. In terms of place names, this is the only memento of the Grey Friars in the City.

The **Austin Friars** – the followers of St Augustine of Hippo, not to be confused with the other St Augustine, who became the first Archbishop of Canterbury – are commemorated in a street between the BANK and LONDON WALL.

The **Carthusians** followed St Bruno, but took their name from Chartreuse in the French Alps, where Bruno had his hermitage. The English word 'Charterhouse' derives from them and anywhere called Charterhouse takes its name from this order. The Carthusians too built a monastery in London, near modern Charterhouse Square; the famous public school, which moved to Surrey in 1872, stood on the site after the monastery had been demolished.

The **Crossed, Crutched** or **Crouched Friars** took their name from their habit of carrying a staff with a cross on top of it. *Crouch*, and thence *crutch*, was a Middle English word for 'cross'; there is no suggestion that the friars either limped or bent down more than anyone else. Like the Black Friars, they gave their name to the area of London surrounding their monastery: Pepys refers to 'going through Crouched Friars' in 1666, over a century after the monastery was destroyed. Not many modern Londoners would know what he was talking about, but there is still a street called Crutched Friars, in the shadow of Fenchurch Street station (see the box *Mainline Stations*, page 130).

The **White Friars** or **Carmelites** took their name from Our Lady of Mount Carmel (or, obviously, from the colour of their habits). They established themselves on the other side of the Fleet River from the Black Friars, and they are still remembered in the names of Carmelite Street and its northern extension, Whitefriars Street, which run between the Victoria Embankment and Fleet Street.

Bow Lane

You can't write a book about this part of London without including a mention of Bow Bells (the bells of the church of St Mary-le-Bow) within earshot of which true cockneys are born. As with many City churches, the current building is the most recent in a succession that has been on the site since Anglo-Saxon times. The Norman version had a series of arches or 'bows' of stone, which can still be seen in the crypt, though they've been painted white and look disappointingly modern. These were an unusual architectural feature at the time – unusual enough to have given their name both to the Court of Arches, an ecclesiastical Court of Appeal which was held here, and ultimately to the church itself. See the box *City Churches*, page 31, for others dedicated to the Virgin Mary.

Bow Lane, in which the church is located, was originally called Cordwainers (shoemakers) Street and later Hosier (stocking-makers) Lane, before taking on the name of its ecclesiastical landmark. A statue of a famous cordwainer, John Smith, who gave up cobbling and went to America, establishing the first permanent English colony at Jamestown, Virginia, in 1607, stands outside. Cordwainers, by the way, were so called because they worked in a type of leather called *cordovan*, manufactured in Córdoba in Spain.

In addition to their cockney connection, Bow Bells were once used to sound the curfew, as a means of keeping the peace: anyone not sitting quietly at home after the bells had rung at nine o'clock at night had to carry a light and to have a good reason for being out and about. In the days before traffic caused a perpetual cacophony in the City, the bells could be heard as far away as HACKNEY Marshes, perhaps 7 kilometres as the crow flies; they are the ones that, according to legend, encouraged Dick Whittington to 'turn again' and become Mayor of London.

There is another Bow Church further east, in the former village of Bow, so named after an arching bridge over the river Lea (see LEYTON/LEYTONSTONE). And see BOW STREET for a further variation on the same theme.

Camomile Street

In common with the adjacent Wormwood Street, this runs along the line of the City wall and was probably an unbuilt-on piece of land just inside it. Left to themselves, camomile and wormwood are both entrepreneurial colonisers of waste ground and both would have been of interest in medieval times as medicinal plants. The availability of useful plants is a recurring feature in ancient place names: see DULWICH for another example.

Cheapside

This was the principal market street of medieval London. The Old English *ceap* and *cipeing* (both pronounced as if they began with *ch*) meant 'market' and several medieval towns, such as Chipping Campden and Chipping Norton, granted the lucrative privilege of holding a market, have a relic of the fact in their names. Although Cheapside literally means 'district beside the market', you can see by looking at a modern map that it cut straight through the middle: streets such as Bread Street and POULTRY run off it. See the box *What You See Is What You Get*, page 45.

Cornhill

No distance from CHEAPSIDE or POULTRY, this was the site of the grain market, situated on the highest hill in the City. The market was an ancient one: Stow refers to it as having been held 'time out of mind'.

Bringing corn to London to make bread for the burgeoning population was given an incentive in the reign of Edward I (1272–1307): carts carrying cheese and corn, or nuts and corn, paid a toll of twopence if the cheese or nuts were worth more than the corn; this was reduced to a halfpenny if the value of the corn was greater. It makes you wonder how the authorities assessed this and how long it took them to check each cart, but presumably somebody thought it was worth it.

The corn market also had special privileges: according to a royal proclamation of 1310, it was the only one permitted to remain open after midday. The dispensation didn't last long, however: the local marketeers took advantage of it to trade in substandard goods after dark, in particular passing off second-hand clothes as new, so in 1369 another edict was passed, forbidding even the Cornhill market from opening after sunset.

The earliest known map of London, dated by experts to 1559, marks this street as 'Cornwell': it had a natural source of fresh water which had been conveyed along it by a stone-built conduit since at least the fourteenth century. Shortly after the map was drawn, in 1582, this was developed into the first mechanically pumped water supply in London.

Cowcross Street

Stow tells us that this was named after a cross that once stood here and, presumably, the vast number of cows that passed by on their way to market at SMITHFIELD. It also, in 1691, boasted a whipping post: public flogging of miscreants was not abolished until the 1830s.

Dowgate Hill

Not all the City 'gates' were in the wall – this was a water gate near the point where the WALBROOK entered the Thames. Stow's spelling, Dunegate, by which he means Downgate, is reasonable enough – the street down to the river is pretty steep – but is probably a misreading of something more like Duva's Gate. If that is the truth, the gate is simply named after a long-forgotten Saxon who owned it, worked it or was in some way connected with it. Dowgate Hill runs into Cousin Lane, derived not from cousins but from several generations of men called William Cosin who lived there in the thirteenth century. Between Cousin Lane and the river is Steelyard Passage, which commemorates an enormous set of scales used to weigh goods as they came into the docks here.

The Steelyard, built on the site of what is now Cannon Street station (see the box *Mainline Stations*, page 130) and first recorded in 1422, was the part of the *Kontor* or trading post of the Hanseatic League. The League, which took its name from an association of over 100 northern German towns and guilds known as the Hanse, was the greatest force in European trade from the thirteenth to the fifteenth centuries, bringing timber, fur, wheat and all manner of other things into England while shipping primarily cloth out across Europe. At its peak it was important enough to alienate rivals and became involved in naval wars with trading powers such as the Dutch and the Burgundians. Think of that as a trade union fighting a country – in a real war, not just a campaign of industrial action – and it will give you some idea of what a punch the Hanse packed. Eventually it grew too big for its boots and collapsed as a result of internal squabbles and the rise of other northern European empires. The London *Kontor* closed in 1598, but Steelyard Passage remains and if you stroll along this stretch of the Thames Path you'll also come across a Hanseatic Walk to remind you of the League's former glories.

Gracechurch Street

This name probably isn't as elegant in origin as it sounds, although it used often to be written 'Gracious Street' and a description of James I's coronation procession in 1604 considered the street to be worthy of the name. Sadly the 'grace' was almost certainly originally 'grass', perhaps because the original church was surrounded by it.

Gracious, Grass Church or whatever you want to call it Street was destroyed in the Great Fire; when it was rebuilt it officially became Gracechurch Street. And what about the church, you may ask? Well, in the nineteenth century, as the City was becoming more of a business district, less of a residential area, congregations fell and land prices rose. Maintaining all the City's historic churches became an expensive luxury. According to John Betjeman (1906–84), Poet Laureate and lover of church architecture, 'Many of Wren's churches were sold by successive bishops of London and the money used for building new churches in the suburbs. Between 1782 and 1939 twenty-six City churches were destroyed, nineteen of them Wren's.' St Benet's, once on the corner of Gracechurch Street and Fenchurch Street (see the box *Mainline Stations*, page 130), was one of the casualties.

CITY CHURCHES

Some of the capital's many churches are named after lesser-known saints: St Botolph, a seventh-century missionary who may have connections with Boston in Lincolnshire (and who has an area of Boston, Massachusetts, named after him); St Ethelburga, first Abbess of BARKING; and St Vedast, a Frankish bishop of the sixth century. Foster is an anglicised version of his name, which is how the City church comes by the wonderful name of St Vedast-alias-Foster. But most of the intriguing names are those given to churches dedicated to 'popular' saints, in order to distinguish them from one another.

St Andrew by the Wardrobe takes its name from its proximity to – yes, really – Edward III's wardrobe. The king (who reigned from 1327 to 1377) moved his gear out of the Tower of London to a building nearby, which became known as the Great Wardrobe. It's an inconvenient distance from the Tower – about 3 kilometres away, near St Paul's – but presumably Edward sent an underling to fetch his robes rather than stroll through the streets of the City in his pyjamas.

St Andrew Undershaft stood, in medieval times, in the shadow of a giant maypole erected each year in nearby CORNHILL. It was, literally, 'under the shaft' of the pole.

St Katharine Cree is a corruption of 'St Katharine's Christ Church', after the twelfth-century priory with which it was associated.

St Margaret Pattens derives the distinctive part of its name from the old-fashioned overshoes called 'pattens' that used to be made and sold nearby. A patten consisted of a wooden sole strapped round the foot and mounted on a metal ring to raise you above the mud of the streets. When you reached your destination you could take the pattens off and display reasonably clean shoes. Although the fashion went out when paved roads came in, a sign in the church to this day requests women to leave their pattens before entering.

St Peter ad Vincula ('in chains') sits within and is the parish church of the Tower of London, although the first known chapel on the site pre-dates the Norman Conquest and is therefore older than the Tower. Strictly speaking being within the precincts of the Tower means that it isn't in the City, but it is close enough for the purposes of this box. St Peter, one of Christ's apostles, was imprisoned by King Herod in Jerusalem, but released by an angel. 'Ad vincula', a Latin reference to this story, is often added to the name of churches dedicated to Peter.

And finally, churches dedicated to the Virgin Mary are probably the most common of all. Those in London include St Mary-le-Bow (see BOW LANE), ST MARY AXE and...

- **St Mary Abchurch** in Abchurch Lane: over the years there have been various suggestions. It may have been a corruption of 'up church', because it was upriver from St Mary Overie in SOUTHWARK or because it stood on rising ground. Modern wisdom prefers the idea that it was connected with a man called Abba, possibly the founder or an early priest.
- **St Mary Aldermary** is traditionally assumed to mean 'older Mary': that is, the oldest Church of St Mary in the City. Certainly there has been a church on the site for 900 years.
- **St Mary-at-Hill** is at the top of a steep hill if you happen to be climbing from BILLINGSGATE Quay up into the medieval city.
- **St Mary Woolnoth** is named after a Saxon noble who established a church here on the site of a Roman temple.

Gresham Street

The Royal Exchange, established in 1565, owes its existence to Sir Thomas Gresham (c. 1519–79), a wealthy merchant who had spent time in Antwerp. The Flemish city boasted a splendid *bourse* or centre of commerce where merchants from all over the world could talk and do business, and Thomas decided that London deserved something similar. The resulting building was opened by Queen Elizabeth, destroyed in the Great Fire, rebuilt, burnt down again, rebuilt again and opened by Queen Victoria. A life crowded with incident, you might say, but it earned its founder the right to have a street named after him just down the hill. William Camden, writing not long after Gresham's death, was obviously a fan, both of the man and of the place: he describes the Exchange as 'a magnificent worke verily, whether you respect the modall of the building, the resort of Merchants from all Nations thither, or the store of wares there'. Lloyds of London traded from here from 1774, with brief intermissions because of fire damage, until they moved to their own building in 1928.

Thomas did rather more for the world than build an Exchange, though: he also founded Gresham College, where the Royal Society held its first meetings and which to this day gives free public lectures on the subjects appointed by him: 'divinity, law, astronomy, music, geometry, rhetoric and physic'.

It's worth mentioning, in the interests of accuracy, that the Royal Exchange isn't in Gresham Street: it sits between THREADNEEDLE STREET and CORNHILL. Gresham Street is further west and the remarkable building in it is the Guildhall, probably where medieval citizens paid their taxes (Old English *gild*) and certainly where the Mayor of London held grand functions and where important state trials, including that of the 'nine-days queen' Lady Jane Grey in 1553, took place. Walk into its Great Hall and you think, 'Yep. It's called great for a reason.' The Guildhall has the distinction of being the only secular stone building still standing in London that pre-dates the Great Fire. We also now know that it was built on the site of the Roman amphitheatre: until 1988 no one was sure that Londinium had one, but it would have been an unusual Roman town if it didn't. The remains – described in the exhibit as fragments, but undeniably substantial fragments – were discovered when the foundations of the new art gallery were being dug and can now be seen, free of charge, by anyone who cares to stroll in.

Leadenhall Street

In the fourteenth century a mansion with a lead roof stood on part of the site of London's first-century forum, the symbolic heart of the Roman city. The name Leadenhall means 'hall with a lead roof', and it is this long-vanished mansion that gave the area its name.

The sequence of events went something like this. Part of the mansion's gardens were converted into an open-air market (conspicuously lacking a lead – or any other – roof), originally just for poultry, then also for cheese and butter and eventually all sorts of other goods too. In 1488 it became the only place in London permitted to sell leather, and in 1622 acquired a monopoly in cutlery. The market was badly damaged in the Great Fire and was replaced with a building of considerable elegance: Strype tells us that:

> Leadenhall is a very large Building of Free Stone, containing within it three large Courts, or Yards, all encompassed with Buildings; wherein is kept a Market, one of the greatest, the best, and the most general for all Provisions in the City of London, nay of the Kingdom; and if I should say of all Europe, I should not give too great a Praise.

That building was in turn replaced in the late nineteenth century, by which time its chief fame lay in the range of poultry available: 'live game and tame fowl, from swans, herons, snipe and pheasants, down to Dorking fowls and the latest novelty in the poultry yard'. You'd be hard pushed to buy a heron there nowadays, but there is still an impressive array of shops and market stalls.

So from the seventeenth to the nineteenth centuries the market was made of stone; the current structure, designed by Horace Jones, who was also responsible for SMITHFIELD and the old BILLINGSGATE markets, is of wrought iron and glass. But hundreds of years after the lead roof ceased to be a feature, the name Leadenhall is still with us.

Lombard Street

A group of merchants called the Lombards – from Lombardy, in northern Italy – settled here in the thirteenth century; it is almost certainly not a coincidence that their success can be traced to the years immediately following Edward I's expulsion of the Jews in 1290 (see CHANCERY LANE and OLD JEWRY). Lombard Street has been the centre of money-lending and banking ever since. In 1873, the econo-mist Walter Bagehot published a book called *Lombard Street: a description of the money market*, one of the 'classic' early works about banking. His title would have been every bit as clear to his audience as 'Wall Street' or 'The City' would be today.

Perhaps the secret of the success of the Lombard Street bankers was that they got plenty of peace and quiet: there was a time when the street was 'paved' with rubber to cut down on the noise of horses' hooves so as not to disturb them. Whether this meant in their negoti-ations or in their post-prandial naps is not specified but it must have been popular: the rubber was re-laid during the Second World War and was still in place in the 1950s, when horses were no longer the most common cause of traffic noise in the City.

London Wall

The original wall around London was built in the second or third century AD and enclosed an area of approximately 130 hectares, about half the traditional 'square mile' of the City. It described a rough semi-circle from the Thames at Blackfriars to the Thames just to the west of the Tower, its northernmost point running along the street that is now called – unsurprisingly – London Wall. It was a massive structure, 6 metres high, 2.5 metres thick and built from 85,000 tonnes of stone shipped up from Kent for the purpose. Archaeology tells us that, after the departure of the Romans, London was largely abandoned – the Saxon settlement was further west, along the STRAND – but by the ninth century it was important enough for the Danes to sack it and for Alfred the Great to bother to rebuild and refortify it. Thereafter, the wall survived more or less intact until the eighteenth century, when the City fathers finally admitted that it was getting in the way of expansion. Even so, impressive chunks of it survive – two of the best can be seen in the gardens of the Museum of London and near Tower Hill tube station. For the gates that led in and out of the old city, see the box *The City Gates* below.

THE CITY GATES

Obviously a walled city needs gates if people are to get in and out. Medieval London had six, echoing the original Roman ones (a seventh, MOORGATE, was added later). They were substantial affairs, offering accommodation to the gatekeepers and, in some cases, serving as prisons. They were sometimes lavishly decorated or, more gruesomely, adorned with the remains of criminals who had been executed: within months of the Restoration of Charles II in 1660, Pepys records seeing 'the limbs of some of our new traytors set upon Aldersgate, which was a sad sight to see' – ten men had been hanged, drawn and quartered in that 'bloody week'. The gates were demolished around 1760 to help cope with increased traffic, but descendants of the Roman thoroughfares that ran through them remain in use to this day and retain the names they had in medieval times. Starting in the west and working clockwise, the gates were:

Ludgate: commemorated in Ludgate Hill (where there is a plaque to mark its site) and Ludgate Circus, this almost certainly means nothing more imaginative than 'back gate' or 'side gate', from the Old English name. However, the twelfth-century chronicler Geoffrey of Monmouth wrote about a King Lud who lived in about the first century BC. Lud, according to Geoffrey, greatly expanded the existing small settlement of London and named it after himself (an Old Celtic version of 'Lud's fortress' would have been something not far removed from 'Luddon'). The trouble with Geoffrey as a chronicler was that he never let the truth get in the way of a good story and this is almost certainly an example of that foible.

Newgate isn't as new as all that: Stow tells us that it was 'latelier built than the rest', but he is talking about the medieval version, which he assigns to the reigns of Henry I (1087–1100) or Stephen (1100–35), a couple of centuries after Alfred the Great had restored the city. There was certainly a gate here in the Roman wall.

Aldersgate was a late addition to the Roman wall, perhaps third or fourth century. The name is Old English and comes from a personal name – at some point in its history, this was 'the gate associated with a man called Ealdred'. A plaque on modern Aldersgate Street marks its site, by Number 62.

It is likely that **Cripplegate** originated not with cripples but with creeping: it may have been a covered passageway running between the BARBICAN and the wall. Folk etymology soon took hold of it, however, so that a church dedicated to St Giles, patron saint of cripples, was built just outside the gate. Ben Jonson, a contemporary of Shakespeare, could safely assume his audience would know what he was talking about when he described a wannabe poet as 'as lame as Vulcan [a crippled Roman god] or the founder of Cripplegate'. There is also a legend that the body of the martyred King Edmund (of Bury St Edmunds fame) was brought here and performed posthumous miracles, enabling the crippled to walk. You can believe that or not, just as you choose.

Although the name **Bishopsgate** post-dates the Romans by several hundred years, their influence can still be seen in the straightness of the road which leads out of the City here: it was the beginning of Ermine Street, which led to the important Roman settlements at Lincoln and York. The gate is named after Earconwald, Bishop of London, who according to tradition rebuilt it in the late seventh century.

Aldgate (not to be confused with Aldersgate) is probably a corruption of 'ale gate', presumably because ale was brewed nearby and sold to travellers entering the City. An alternative suggestion is that it was 'all gate', that is, a gate for all, because, unlike Bishopsgate, you could pass through it without payment of a fee. The modern spelling, suggesting 'old gate', appears in the seventeenth century and when you think about it is quite silly, because all these gates were pretty old by then.

Lothbury

This oddly named street lies on part of a medieval manor (Old English *burh*) that once belonged to a man called Hlotha, about whom we know nothing other than that he owned a manor hereabouts. Stow says that the name was recorded as Lethbury in Edward III's time (1327–77) and that Lothbury is a corruption; but as he later records having seen it written Lothburie, Lathburie and Loadburie, that only proves the randomness of spelling in those days (see BARBICAN for a rare exception to this general rule).

Stow also tells us that the Founders (metal workers) were based here, which lends some support to the alternative theory that the name was originally Lottenbury, meaning 'manor of the candlestick makers'. The problem is that *–bury* is an odd ending in this context. It is more likely that someone made this up rather than give credit to the unknown Hlotha.

Mansion House

Sounds like a tautology, doesn't it? What could a mansion be other than a house?

The Mansion House is the official residence of the Lord Mayor of London, built in the eighteenth century on the site of the old Stocks

Market (so called because it was in turn built over a place where there had once been stocks, of the kind people used to sit in as a public punishment for petty crimes). At the end of the thirteenth century it was a meat and fish market; it was burnt down during the Great Fire and replaced with a market selling 'Fruits, Roots, and Herbs; for which it is very considerable and much resorted unto, being of note for having the choicest in their kind of all sorts, surpassing all the other markets in London'. That's according to Strype, writing before COVENT GARDEN took over the fruit and veg franchise. Anyway, the Stocks Market moved to FARRINGDON STREET in 1737, leaving the site vacant for the Lord Mayor's residence.

None of which explains why it ended up with this odd name. Well, 'mansion house' is not in fact a tautology; it is a technical term meaning 'official residence'. It was used originally in ecclesiastical circles to mean a house that went with the job and, although that sense is now obsolete, it does describe exactly what the Mansion House is – the house that goes with the job of being Lord Mayor.

Monument

The Monument at Monument commemorates the Great Fire of 1666, which according to tradition started in a bakery in nearby Pudding Lane and ended way over the other side of St Paul's, at PIE CORNER. Designed by Christopher Wren and Robert Hooke, the monument was originally to have had a phoenix on the top – the phoenix being a bird that rose again from its own ashes. Wren then thought better of his own idea (costly, difficult to interpret from a distance and dangerous 'by reason of the sail the spread wings will carry in the wind') and the existing vase of flames was substituted.

At 61.6 metres (202 feet), the Monument is now dwarfed by more recent City buildings, but is still the tallest free-standing column in the world, towering 10 metres above Nelson in TRAFALGAR SQUARE and almost double the height of Trajan's Column in Rome. The location was chosen because it was the nearest convenient one to the infamous Pudding Lane bakery; it was, ironically, the site of a church that had been destroyed by the fire. It is usually said that the memorial was made 202 feet tall because that was the distance from site to bakery, but it was also a convenient height for Wren and Hooke to use it as a telescope and measure the position of the stars. They conducted their experiments in the lower reaches of the Monument, and you can still look down through a grille at the bottom of the staircase and see the cellar where they worked. There isn't really anything to see, but it does have the advantage that you don't have to climb the famous 311 narrow winding steps to reach it. And, to tie up one last loose end, the Monument itself is referred to with a definite article; the tube station is merely Monument.

Old Bailey

In the traditional Norman castle, the bailey was the outer wall, protecting the motte or mound on which the inner keep was built. This little street, running between Ludgate and Newgate (see the box *The City Gates*, page 37), didn't protect a castle as such, but was part of the outer fortifications of the City. It was known as the Bailey (in various spellings) as early as the thirteenth century and as the Old Bailey by the sixteenth. Some form of criminal court was also here in the sixteenth century. In the 1830s the courthouse became the Central Criminal Court and its jurisdiction was extended beyond the City of London and the County of Middlesex so that it could try those from farther afield whose notoriety meant they were unlikely to receive a fair hearing on their home turf.

Old Jewry

Not the most politically correct name in the book, but a fairly self-explanatory one: 'an area where Jews used to live'. Edward I expelled the Jews from England in 1290 (see CHANCERY LANE), so this street has been an 'old' or former Jewish quarter since that ignoble date.

An interesting sideline here for anyone who has ever struggled with the morality of *The Merchant of Venice*. Christian law at the time forbade anyone from lending money and charging interest; Jewish law did not, and there was no religious objection to Jews making 'business loans' to Christians. So non-Jews could have it both ways: they could take the money and still despise the Shylocks of their world for behaving in an 'unchristian' way.

Paternoster Square

Pater noster is Latin for 'our father', the first two words of the Lord's Prayer (which continues 'which art in Heaven…'). Catholics 'saying the rosary' begin with this prayer and move on to the Hail Mary or *Ave Maria*. People who made rosaries were called paternosterers and in the early fourteenth century there was a Paternoster Street (later Row) adjacent to St Paul's where many of them went about their business. In later years the paternosterers gave way to stationers and booksellers and at the end of the seventeenth century the street had a complete revamp, with – according to Daniel Defoe – 'spacious shops, back-warehouses, skylights and other conveniences' being built specifically for the Mercers, a wealthy band of tradesmen who dealt in fine fabrics. Paternoster Square was built on the site of nearby Newgate Market in the late nineteenth century and has been part of the recent facelift of the precincts of St Paul's.

The Christian theme is continued nearby in Ave Maria Lane, where 'text-writers and bead-makers' once traded; in Creed Lane, where 'all sorts of books then in use, namely, A B C, with the Pater Noster, Ave, Creed, Graces, etc.' were sold in Elizabethan times; and Amen Corner, where religious texts were also sold. In 1831 the clergyman and wit Sydney Smith took up an appointment as canon at St Paul's, which provided him with accommodation. He wrote, 'The house is in Amen Corner – an awkward name on a card, and an awkward annunciation to the coachman on leaving a fashionable mansion.' Think how much more embarrassed he'd have been had he lived to see his address adopted as the name of a 1960s pop group.

Poultry

In the great market that seemed to occupy much of medieval London, streets were named for practicality and ease of shopping (see box *What You See Is What You Get*, page 45). So no prizes for guessing what was originally sold on Poultry. By Stow's time, however, 'men of trades and sellers of wares…have oftentimes since changed their places, as they have found their best advantage'. He follows this with an intriguing list of people who have moved: 'the pepperers and grocers of Soper's Lane are now in Bucklersbury and other places dispersed', for example, but 'the brewers for the more part remain near the friendly waters of Thames…poulterers of late [have] removed out of the Poultry, betwixt the stocks and the great conduit in Cheap, into Grass Street and St Nicholas Shambles.' The shambles were traditionally the butchers' area, so this may indicate some overlap, but it was also presumably a matter of going where rents were cheap and customers were near at hand.

An early meaning of the word *poultry* was 'a market where fowl are sold', which explains why this street was always called The Poultry, never Poultry Street. The OED tells us that this is the oldest recorded and only surviving use of the word in this sense.

WHAT YOU SEE IS WHAT YOU GET

As we saw under POULTRY, the naming of the market streets in medieval London was basic and self-explanatory: in the area around CHEAPSIDE we still find Bread Street, Milk Street, Goldsmiths' Street and Ironmonger Lane, reflecting the occupations of people who lived and worked there hundreds of years ago. Garlick Hill even retains the old spelling. There is a Fish Street Hill down near the MONUMENT and a Stew Lane, suggesting not casseroles but brothels, near SOUTHWARK Bridge. Like the brewers mentioned under Poultry, the fishmongers of Fish Street Hill stayed where they were when other traders were moving around, as they were conveniently situated for the fish market at BILLINGSGATE. Further out of town, bricks and tiles were made in Brick Lane.

Two names that might once have been self-explanatory but now perhaps need more investigation are Distaff Street and Friday Street. A distaff is a device used in spinning – it's the spool round which the thread is wound as it is spun. So the residents of Distaff Street earned their living by spinning. It is because this was predominantly a woman's occupation that we have the expression 'the distaff side' of the family, meaning the female line.

Opinions vary about Friday Street. I like Stow's idea that it was the site of an old fish market, Friday being the day when Christians traditionally abstained from meat and ate fish instead. Sadly, this is probably not entirely true. It is possible that the street was the site of a Friday market, not necessarily devoted to fish, or that it was associated with someone called

Frigedaeg, perhaps because he was born on a Friday. Stow's fish connection certainly held sway for forty years after he compiled his survey: Ben Jonson's *Masque of Christmas*, first performed in 1616, has a joke about people from both Friday Street and Fish Street being 'not Christmas creatures' because they are associated with fasting.

Cloak Lane may be another deceptive name: it's possible that it comes from the Latin *cloaca* and means that a sewer used to run along it. But Stow refers to it as Horseshoe Bridge Street, after a bridge over the WALBROOK, built over by his time but probably named because of its vaulted shape. Strype, writing 120 years later, refers to Cloak Lane without comment or explanation and, as Wheatley in the nineteenth century says, 'it is not likely in later times to have been called Cloak Lane from an *ancient* sewer'. So maybe someone in the seventeenth century *did* sell cloaks there. It's hard to be sure.

For an example of something where what you see is *not* what you get, see SHOE LANE.

St Mary Axe

This street is famous nowadays as the home of 'the Gherkin'; the church after which it is named no longer exists. 'Axe' is said to derive from a relic possessed by the church, one of the axes used by the Huns to behead 11,000 virgins who were followers of St Ursula. Considering that this atrocity took place in Cologne, you may wonder how the axe ended up in London, but early Christian relics are known to have covered a lot of ground and attracted a lucrative trade in visiting pilgrims. For other churches dedicated to the Virgin Mary, see the box *City Churches,* page 31.

Threadneedle Street

As readers of the biblical Book of Genesis will know, Adam and Eve, on realising that they were naked, 'sewed fig leaves together and made themselves aprons'. This quotation has for many centuries formed the motto of the Needlemakers' Guild, whose coat of arms shows the modestly clad Adam and Eve supporting a shield on which are depicted three needles crowned with coronets. Sewing – and therefore needlemaking – we deduce, is as old as time.

The Needlemakers were and are one of the so-called livery companies that emerged from the medieval guilds, an early form of trade association dedicated to maintaining high standards within their trade or craft. Among other things they were responsible for training apprentices, controlling imports and regulating wages and working conditions. Today there are over 100 of them, ranging from the Armourers & Brasiers to the Information Technologists, though the latter don't claim to date back to the Middle Ages. In 1515, the Court of Aldermen of the City of London ranked the companies in an order of precedence that continues in force to this day (although it is reviewed periodically to accommodate the likes of the Information Technologists).

According to this list, the Needlemakers (no disrespect intended) are rather small beer. They rank sixty-fifth and have never had their own hall. Nevertheless, it is possible that the three needles on their shield are the origin of Threadneedle Street.

Alternatively, the name could derive from the activities of the rather grander Merchant Taylors, whose splendid headquarters have been in the street since the fourteenth century. The Worshipful Company of Merchant Taylors was one of the twelve 'great' livery companies of medieval London. It ranks either sixth or seventh in the order of precedence (there's an ongoing dispute with the Skinners about this) and it grew into a large philanthropic organisation that endowed the schools called Merchant Taylors found throughout the country. But its members were originally tailors and linen-armourers (the latter made the padded tunics worn under suits of armour) and, obviously, used needles and threads.

So you have a choice: three needles or thread and needle? Stow, one of the first to record the name, spells it 'three', but 'thread' appears not much later. It's impossible to be sure which is right.

Lovers of old-fashioned slang will know that the Old Lady of Threadneedle Street is the BANK of England. The bank has had its headquarters here since 1734; the nickname was in popular use by the end of that century.

Throgmorton Street

Sir Nicholas Throckmorton or Throgmorton (in a time when most people were illiterate it would have been easy to confuse the two) was an Elizabethan politician and diplomat, much involved in the wheeling and dealing between Elizabeth and Mary Queen of Scots. His career suffered when he was rumoured to be on Mary's side – in a nutshell Mary claimed to be the rightful queen of England and there were plots aplenty to depose Elizabeth in her favour. There were also official negotiations to make Mary Elizabeth's heir.

In a nationwide atmosphere of deep paranoia, many people were routinely suspected of treason; Nick, who seems to have been remarkably outspoken for a career diplomat, spent some time in the Tower, but was never brought to trial. He died in 1571 after a year or two of ill health. It has been rumoured that he was poisoned by Elizabeth's favourite, the Earl of Leicester, but the *Dictionary of National Biography* says austerely that 'no reliance need be placed on this report'.

This street is named after him, though with all his gadding about France, Scotland and his own estates in the Midlands, he can't have spent much time there.

Walbrook

As the name suggests, this used to be a stream, running down between the twin peaks of Ludgate Hill (see the box *The City Gates*, page 37) and CORNHILL and meeting the Thames beside what is now Cannon Street station (see the box *Mainline Stations*, page 130); the modern street called Walbrook follows roughly this course. *Wal–* comes from the same Old English root as Wales and many other place names; it means Britons, Celts or simply 'foreigners' and was used by the Anglo-Saxons to denote the people who had lived in a place before them. Which may mean that there were still Celts living in this area when the Anglo-Saxons arrived and settled to the west of the City.

Stow tells us that the Walbrook was once 'a fair brook of sweet water', but that was a good bit before his time. In 1374 (200 years before Stow) Edward III leased some land north of the City to a brewer named Thomas atte Ram. In the lease was the proviso that he 'shall have the Watercourse of Walbrook cleansed for the whole of the term aforesaid; and shall have the same cleared of dung and other filth thrown or deposited therein'. As a reward for his efforts, Thomas was to be allowed to keep and make use of any of the said dung or filth, some of which would doubtless have been useful as fuel.

This brook-turned-sewer had been entirely covered over by the end of the sixteenth century, but Walbrook retained a more savoury claim to fame: according to the first ever book of English common law, produced in the fifteenth century and known as the *Liber Albus* or *White Book*, certain sorts of trial required a jury of thirty-six reputable men. Because the Walbrook was deemed to run down the middle of the City, that jury had to be composed of eighteen men from the east side and eighteen from the west.

WITHOUT THE WALL

There is an electoral ward in the City of London called FARRINGDON Within and another called Farringdon Without, a distinction dating from the fourteenth century and indicating that one was inside and the other outside the City walls. This usage crops up with London churches, too – there is a St Botolph without Bishopsgate and a St Sepulchre without Newgate, both just outside where those historic gates once stood (see the box *The City Gates*, page 37). This section therefore concerns the outer parts of the modern City. Some of them grew up as London expanded; others deliberately started life away from the restrictions imposed by the City fathers.

Barbican

Camden tells us that this is an Arabic word, but modern dictionaries are not so sure. From an uncertain source it found its way into English via Old French and was in use here by the end of the thirteenth century. Amazingly, the Elizabethan poet Edmund Spenser, whose spelling matches that of Winnie the Pooh for wobbliness, spelt it in the modern way in 1590. I suppose the law of averages would tell us that even he must sometimes get something right.

Anyway, according to the OED, *barbican* means 'an outer fortification or defence to a city or castle, especially a double tower erected over a gate or bridge; often made strong and lofty, and serving as a watch-tower' and that is precisely what the London barbican was. Stow calls it a *burhkenning* or watchtower, spelling it as if it derived from Old English, but that is almost certainly the result of a popular attempt to anglicise an unfamiliar word.

Henry III (1216–72) had the original barbican pulled down at the end of his war with the barons in 1267, presumably as a gesture of peace and goodwill, or perhaps to stop his former enemies getting their hands on it. Over the centuries other buildings on the same site came and went until the area was badly bombed during the Second World War, leaving the way free for the development of the modern arts and conference centre.

Bridewell Place/St Bride's

The first item of importance in this area was the well – doubtless there in pagan times, but in the early Christian era 'taken over' by the Irish St Bride or Bridget. There has been a church here since the sixth century, possibly founded by Irish missionaries who were doing their bit in Britain before St Augustine set foot in Canterbury in 597.

In any event, first you have the well, then you have the church. Then Henry VIII built a palace on the riverbank, by what is now BLACKFRIARS Bridge – as several references in this book show, he was almost as keen on building palaces as he was on destroying monasteries. Henry's son Edward VI, a lad of less extravagant habits, donated it in 1553 to the City of London, who promptly turned it into a prison, workhouse and house of correction 'for the strumpet and idle person, for the rioter that consumeth all, and for the vagabond that will abide in no place'. This worthy intention backfired because, as one later writer puts it, 'idle and abandoned people from the outskirts of London and parts adjacent, under colour of seeking an asylum in the new institution, settled in London in great numbers, to the great annoyance of the graver residents'. The asylum was converted into a grain store, presumably putting all the vagrants and strumpets out on the streets, which can't have pleased the graver residents either; it then burned down in the Great Fire. It was rebuilt and continued in use as, variously, a workhouse, a training ground for apprentices and a prison for minor offenders until the mid-nineteenth century.

In the meantime, the present church of St Bride's had been designed after the fire by Christopher Wren. Its multi-layered steeple was intended to be visible from the Fleet River (see FLEET STREET). Certainly it was visible from the workplace of one William Rich, apprentice baker in Ludgate Hill, who, being about to marry the boss's daughter, concocted a wedding cake to look like the church – and established a template for every wedding-cake maker since. Difficult to imagine now, but images from about this time (the mid-eighteenth century) show that St Bride's was a significant landmark: it and St Paul's were the only tall buildings around.

Chancery Lane

Originally known by the less memorable title of New Street, Chancery Lane became famous in the thirteenth century as the location of a House of Converts, founded by Henry III (1216–72) for the specific purpose of converting Jews to Christianity. The name New Street was therefore abandoned in favour of Converts or Convers Lane. Then Edward I (1272–1307) decided that even converted Jews were not wanted in his kingdom: he expelled them *en masse*. Yes, really

– incredible though it may sound, it was illegal for Jews to worship in public in England until 1656, when Oliver Cromwell, with an eye on wealthy Jewish businessmen who had congregated in Amsterdam after being expelled from Spain and Portugal by the Inquisition, rescinded Edward's decree (see BEVIS MARKS).

Anyway, the house of conversion being surplus to requirements, it came into the hands of the Custos Rotulorum or Master of the Rolls, whose job was to keep the records of the Court of Chancery, a now defunct division of English and Welsh law. The word *chancery* derives from *chancellor* and for several centuries the Master of the Rolls also held the title of Lord Chancellor: Henry VII's influential adviser John Morton was one, and Henry VIII's Thomas Cromwell (of *Wolf Hall* fame) another. Thus within a generation of the departure of the Jews, the street came to be known as Chancellor's Lane and by the fifteenth century had been corrupted into its current form.

Farringdon Road/Farringdon Street

Farringdon is an Old English name meaning 'ferny hill' and it is found in London thanks to two distinguished goldsmiths of that name, father-in-law and son-in-law, who were sheriffs and aldermen in the thirteenth century. See also the introduction to this section, page 50.

Fetter Lane

Although frequently the scene of public executions, Fetter Lane seems to have nothing to do with fetters, but rather with what Chaucer calls *faitours* and Stow *fewters*. Either way it means idlers or vagrants. The name goes back to at least the fourteenth century, when official documents show that the powers that be were anxious to clean up the place. Get rid of the layabouts, bring in a gallows – you can see how that would raise the tone.

Fleet Street

Contrary to popular belief, the river Fleet ran not along modern Fleet Street but at right angles to it, along FARRINGDON Road and New Bridge Street and down into the Thames. It had quite a broad estuary and there were two islands in the middle of it, near what is now Ludgate Circus (see the box *The City Gates*, page 37): we know that the Romans built at least one bridge across the Fleet at this point. By the seventeenth century the river was sluggish, noisome and full of who knows what sort of undesirable rubbish; the section from the Thames up to HOLBORN was made into a 12-metre wide canal under the auspices of Sir Christopher Wren, who took time out from rebuilding churches after the Great Fire to act as London's Surveyor General with responsibility for all public buildings. And canals. Somehow the canal never attracted the shipping traffic that would have made it commercially viable and in 1766, as *The London Encyclopaedia* graphically tells us, 'soon after a drunken butcher had fallen in and, unable to extricate himself from the mud, had frozen to death, the rest of the Fleet was covered over and so became an underground sewer instead of an open one'.

All that said, Fleet Street has been there a long time. It was recorded as Fleet Bridge Street as early as 1228 and 'Fleet Street, in the suburbs of London' in 1311. The word comes from the Old English for 'stream, pool or creek', so was a pretty basic name to give to a slow-flowing river that was much smaller than the nearby Thames.

Houndsditch

This was originally literally a ditch, part of the moat on the outer side of the Roman wall. By the late sixteenth century it had been filled in, but Stow tells us that it took its name 'for that in olde time when the same lay open, much filth (conueyed forth of the Citie) especially dead Dogges were there layd or cast'. A nineteenth-century chronicler reports that although there were indeed dogs in the ditch, it is likely that they were alive and well: the kennels housing the dogs used for 'the City hunts' were kept there. No one seems to be sure which version is true – it is even possible that Houndsditch comes from an Anglo-Saxon personal name, as HOUNSLOW does, but this seems undesirably prosaic by comparison with the other two suggestions.

Minories

The Minoresses were nuns who belonged to an order founded by St Clare and St Francis and who built a nunnery on the fringes of the City of London in 1293. The slight corruption of their name came to be used for the surrounding district and survived the dissolution of the abbey under Henry VIII. See also the box *The Friars*, page 25.

Moorgate

This name appears on the earliest known map of London, dated to 1559, but Moorgate wasn't a gate in Roman times (see the box *The City Gates*, page 37, for those that were). It was built in 1415, making the number of gates in the wall up to seven – everyone's favourite lucky number in those days. It takes its name from the moor or marsh that lay outside the walls. By 1559 this had been drained to leave an area marked on the map as Moor Field, which is still the name of the famous eye hospital founded here in 1805. Moorgate was demolished, along with the others, in the early 1760s; the street named after it was built in the 1840s to improve access to the new London Bridge (see the box on *Mainline Stations*, page 130).

Petticoat Lane

In ancient times, says Strype, who was born nearby, the former Hog's Lane had 'hedge rows and elm trees, with pleasant fields to walk in'. And, presumably, pigs being driven along it on their way to pasture or to market. It was then built up, boasting during James I's reign (1603–25) at least two large and elegant houses, one occupied by the Spanish ambassador and the other by the king's jeweller. By this time pigs had given way to a thriving trade in second-hand clothes and the name changed to reflect the fact. The clothing industry in the area was perpetuated by various waves of immigrants, including Huguenot silk-weavers and Jewish tailors, and Petticoat Lane became famous as one of London's largest markets.

The street officially became Middlesex Street in the 1830s, because it marked the boundary between the City of London and the County of Middlesex. Nevertheless, the name of the market – which during the week takes place in nearby Wentworth Street (named, by Strype's time, after a local landowner) and spills over into the former Petticoat Lane only on Sunday mornings – persists.

Pie Corner

Famous as the place where the Great Fire ended (see MONUMENT), this was in the early seventeenth century a place where sustaining food was to be found: a 1641 description of the great Bartholomew Fair refers to 'the Pig Market, alias Pasty Nook, or Pie Corner; where pigs are all hours of the day on the stalls piping hot, and would say (if they could speak) come eat me'. The point where the fire ended is marked by a gilt statue of a fat boy, representing gluttony, because there was a school of thought that God had sent the fire to punish Londoners for this particular sin. Whether these moralists drew their conclusion from the fact that the fire had begun in Pudding Lane and ended in Pie Corner, or whether that is just a happy coincidence, is a question that remains open to debate.

The moralists would have looked pretty silly if that had been their reasoning, though: the origins of Pie (or Pye) Corner have nothing to do with pies. Instead the name refers back to a court known as Piepowders, set up at fairs and markets to resolve disputes involving itinerant traders. Piepowders derives from the French *pieds poudrés*, 'dusty feet', emphasising that those hauled up before the court came from some distance away and so were by definition untrustworthy. There's also a sixteenth-century French idiom *avoir les pieds poudreux*, 'to leave without paying', which is almost certainly connected to the same prejudices.

Pie Corner stands on the corner of the enticingly named Giltspur Street. Stow tells us that this used to be called Knightriders Street, because knights rode this way to the tournaments that were once held in SMITHFIELD. While it is tempting to suggest that the knights were wearing golden spurs (they might have been – these jousting matches were pretty flashy), it is more likely that a number of spur makers once had their workshops here and that one or more of them had the sign of a gilt spur over his premises.

The puddings of Pudding Lane were, sadly, not of the sticky toffee variety: the word refers to the offal of animals that had been butchered in the City markets and were carried down this lane to the river, where they were loaded on to barges and taken away to be disposed of.

Shoe Lane

Nothing to do with shoemakers – who were based in Cordwainers' Street (see BOW LANE) – but possibly something to do with shoes. Early forms of the name show it ending in a version of *land* rather than *lane*, indicating that it may have been 'land given to a monastic community to provide it with shoes'. However, there is an alternative suggestion that it is named after an ancient well, known as the Sho or Scho Well, at the end of the street. This would also probably have come from the Old English for *shoe*, but no one seems very clear why.

One thing we can be sure about, though – the shoemakers of Cordwainers' Street conducted their business bang in the centre of the market area. Shoe Lane, which is inside the modern City but outside the old City walls, would have been quite a trek for someone who needed to have their shoes repaired or replaced.

Smithfield

This famous market was originally called Smoothfield, a plain grassy area just outside the City walls where there was a livestock market in at least the twelfth and probably as early as the tenth century. The fact that horses were sold here may have caused a confusion between 'smooth' and 'smith'. Both Shakespeare and Stow – who were rough contemporaries – use the modern spelling and Falstaff is disparaging about the quality of the horses to be bought there. So is Dryden, nearly a century later:

> *This town two bargains has not worth one farthing,*
> *A Smithfield horse – and wife of Covent Garden.*

He means, of course, that a lady picked up in COVENT GARDEN in those days would have been no lady.

Over the years the market – by now right in the middle of the City – grew to unmanageable levels. The livestock, mostly sheep and cattle, became such a traffic hazard that a new road had to be built to accommodate them (see EUSTON ROAD). Smithfield was also a Health and

Safety nightmare for both animals and people, particularly as much of the required butchery was carried out on the spot. In 1855 it was closed down, the livestock was moved out to ISLINGTON and in due course the current buildings, coping only with animals that are already dead, were erected on the original site.

Spitalfields

Spital is a corruption of 'hospital'; the hospital of St Mary Spital was founded here in the twelfth century, with an impoverished suburb growing up around it. The hospital was closed down by Henry VIII, but its name persisted. In the seventeenth century a market in the locality was licensed to sell 'flesh, fowl and roots' (but not herbs or flowers, you notice – another example of the authorities being very strict about markets) to the ever-increasing population. The restrictions on what could be sold were eventually relaxed to accommodate the Huguenot silk weavers who based themselves in the area and the market grew in importance and diversity. Its fortunes waxed and waned with the wealth or otherwise of the district; the fruit and veg moved east to new premises on the fringes of HACKNEY Marshes in 1991, but the rest of the market has been revitalised and is still to be found on the site it has occupied since 1638. The Hackney branch is, inevitably, called New Spitalfields, despite the fact that its new site has nothing to do with either hospital or fields.

Temple Bar

This was once – from at least the early fourteenth century – a literal metal bar or chain that separated what is now the STRAND from FLEET STREET and, as such, marked the boundary of the City of London in medieval times. The City's (often very strict) jurisdiction did not extend beyond this point. The bar is said to have been erected by the Knights Templar and was close to their church (see the box *In the Name of the Law*, page 139), hence the name. Other roads leading out of London – HOLBORN, for one – had similar bars that have long since been removed.

By Strype's time Temple Bar had been replaced by 'a House of Timber, erected cross the street, with a narrow gateway'; this was removed, presumably for Health and Safety reasons, after the Great Fire and replaced with an elegant stone gate said to have been designed by Wren. This in turn was removed to ease traffic flow in the 1870s; in 1880 the current statue was erected; it has (inevitably) a statue of Queen Victoria in one of its niches and is topped by a heraldic dragon.

The Wren gate, however, has recently been taken out of retirement and has been restored and re-erected in PATERNOSTER SQUARE.

WESTMINSTER SOUTH

The City of Westminster is a strange shape, reaching up farther into the north west than many people realise, while at the same time excluding famous central areas such as BLOOMSBURY and FITZROVIA, which are in the borough of CAMDEN. As I said in the Introduction, some of the boundaries between districts are a little blurry, so let's start with an area about which there can be little argument: Westminster itself.

WESTMINSTER

Archaeological evidence tells us that the Saxons built a monastery to the west of Lundenwìc, on the isle of THORNEY. The mastermind behind this may have been Offa, the eighth-century king of Mercia after whom the dike on the English/Welsh border is named (though there is a reference to him describing the area as an unhealthy marshy slum, which tends to argue against this). But the man responsible for creating London's second city and ensuring that royalty and government focused on this westerly point for ever more was the Saxon king Edward the Confessor (1042–66). It was he who built a palace (long since lost) on a site from which the river had retreated so that it was no longer an island, and restored the old monastery to an ambitious specification. Of this, only the tiny Chapel of the Pyx remains, but over the centuries Edward's project evolved into Westminster Abbey: 'the abbey on the site of the monastery in the west'.

Artillery Row

Strype describes 'a passage into the New Artillery Ground, a pretty large enclosure, made use of by those that delight in military exercises' and in the nineteenth century Mackenzie Walcott's *Memorials of Westminster* tells us that 'upon the spot now occupied by Artillery Place the men of Westminster used to practise at "the butts", which were provided by the parish in obedience to an ordinance of Queen Elizabeth'. 'Butts', of course, were used for archery – see NEWINGTON BUTTS/NEWINGTON CAUSEWAY for further evidence of Elizabeth I's interest in this activity. By Strype's time the archers had moved on and guns moved in.

Big Ben

Not a place as such, but so much a part of everyone's image of London that it seems wrong to leave it out. Strictly speaking Big Ben is the bell in the clock tower at the northern end of the Houses of Parliament, but all except the most pedantic use the term to refer to the tower and the clock as well. The original Ben may have been Sir Benjamin Hall, Chief Commissioner of Works when the bell was cast in the 1850s, or a boxing champion of the time, Benjamin Caunt, whose nickname was 'Big Ben'.

Broad Sanctuary/Little Sanctuary

If you've read or seen *The Hunchback of Notre Dame* (even in Disney cartoon form), you will be familiar with the concept of sanctuary: it meant that you could take refuge in a sacred place, as Quasimodo did with Esmeralda, and the law couldn't touch you. Anyone who violated sanctuary (that is, went in and took somebody out by force) could be excommunicated, as even a criminal who sought sanctuary was believed to take on the sanctity of the place in which he was hiding. The concept was designed to protect the weak and to prevent the abuse of power, though it was much exploited by those who wanted to avoid creditors as well as those who had fallen foul of the king.

Broad and Little Sanctuary once lay within the precincts of Westminster Abbey and most famously gave their protection to Edward IV's queen, Elizabeth Woodville (c. 1437–92), and her children during two crises in her fortunes in the course of the Wars of the Roses. (It's all in Philippa Gregory's *The White Queen*, in case you're intimidated by nineteenth-century French novels, or terrified by Disney cartoons.)

Surprisingly perhaps, the practice of criminals seeking sanctuary in order to escape justice survived Henry VIII's plundering of the monasteries and was not abolished until almost 100 years later, under James I.

THE DEANS OF WESTMINSTER

Stroll around the back streets near Westminster Abbey and you will see any number of streets named after Deans you have never heard of. Most of them were Deans of Westminster Abbey, overseeing the spiritual life of the church.

- **Dean Trench Street** Richard Trench (Dean 1856–64) moved from Westminster to spend the last twenty years of his life as Bishop of Dublin.

- **Dean Stanley Street** Arthur Stanley (Dean 1864–81) was a controversially liberal churchman who offended many contemporaries by expressing the view that 'the Church of England, by the very condition of its being, was not High or Low, but Broad, and had always included and been meant to include, opposite and contradictory opinions'. He was a highly respected teacher, including his successor among his pupils.

- **Dean Bradley Street** George Bradley (Dean 1881–1902) seems to have had no greater claim to fame than that he wrote a biography of his mentor.

- **Dean Ryle Street** Herbert Ryle (Dean 1911–25) was instrumental, just after the First World War, in introducing the Tomb of the Unknown Warrior. He composed the inscription on the tomb which begins 'Beneath this stone rests the body of a British warrior, unknown by name or rank, brought from France to lie among the most illustrious of the land' and also includes the words 'Thus are commemorated the many multitudes who during the great war of 1914–1918 gave the most that man can give – life itself.' This is the only tomb in the Abbey on which – as a sign of respect – you are not allowed to walk.

- **Dean Farrar Street** Frederic W. Farrar (1831–1903) was never actually Dean of Westminster, though he was at various times Rector of St Margaret's (the church next door), archdeacon of the Abbey and Dean of Canterbury. Lovers of Victorian literature may remember him as the author of *Eric, or Little by Little*, which was once up there with *Tom Brown's Schooldays* as an improving tale for young readers.

Also a Dean of Westminster (1802-15) was William Vincent, who had previously been headmaster of Westminster School and who, when the area was being encroached on by developers, paid for 5 hectares of land to become the school's playing fields. Known now as Vincent Square, the land serves the same purpose to this day and is the largest privately owned square in London.

DEAN STREET in Soho also has an ecclesiastical connection, but not to Westminster.

Downing Street

.The street which has housed the Prime Minister's official residence since 1732 takes its name from Sir George Downing (1623–84), who developed the street and built himself a house here. Strype, who was obviously the most appalling snob, described it as 'a pretty open Place, especially at the upper End, where are 4 or 5 very large and well built Houses, fit for Persons of Honour and Quality'. It would be interesting to hear whether he thought some of its more recent residents merited that description.

Great George Street

Designed as an approach to ST JAMES'S Park from WESTMINSTER Bridge during the reign of George II (1727–60), this was named in the king's honour. But its real feature of interest is that it covered over a grubby thoroughfare with the self-explanatory name of Thieving Lane. For more about the slovenliness of Westminster in those days, see TOTHILL STREET.

Greycoat Place/Greencoat Place

The Grey Coat Hospital School opened in a converted workhouse in 1701. Its first pupils were poor children, forty boys and forty girls, and the school's aim was to take them off the streets of the slums around Westminster and turn them into 'loyal citizens, useful workers and solid Christians'. Making them wear grey uniforms was part of the programme. The school still exists, as a Church of England comprehensive for girls, in Greycoat Place and you can see statues of two early pupils, the boy in a grey coat, the girl in a long grey dress, in niches on either side of the entrance. (The boy looks bizarrely like an eighteenth-century version of Harry Potter.)

The Greencoat School – you'll notice a recurring theme in the names – was even older, founded in 1633 'for the relief of the poor fatherless children of St Margaret's Westminster'. Charles I gave £50 a year for its support. Towards the end of the nineteenth century it amalgamated with other charitable schools (there were Brown Coats and Blue Coats too) to form Westminster City School; an idea of what the original uniform was like is displayed in the pub sign of the nearby Greencoat Boy.

It's worth mentioning here that the word 'hospital' in this context is more allied to 'hospitality' than to its modern medical sense. In the seventeenth and eighteenth centuries a hospital – and the Foundling Hospital discussed under CORAM'S FIELDS was another – took in the needy whether they were ill or not.

Horseferry Road

Until the eighteenth century, when first PUTNEY and then WESTMINSTER Bridges were built, there was, between London Bridge and KINGSTON, no way of crossing the river except by boat. From London Bridge to

Kingston is nearly 20 kilometres as the crow flies, very much more if you follow the meandering course of the Thames. Over much of this distance the ferrymen held sway: one of the reasons it took so long to build a bridge at Westminster, which had been a seat of royalty and legislators since before the Norman Conquest, was that the ferrymen were a powerful lobby who thought a bridge would undermine their trade.

From at least the early sixteenth century until 1750, there was only one horse ferry licensed on the Thames. It did a roaring trade carrying passengers and horses back and forth across the river near what is now LAMBETH Bridge, at the bottom of the road that bears its name. A man and a horse paid two shillings, a coach drawn by six horses two shillings and sixpence. The rights to this ferry and the income from it belonged to the Archbishop of Canterbury, whose official residence, Lambeth Palace, was and is just across the river. When the ferry trade fell away after the construction of Westminster Bridge, the archbishop was paid £3,000 in compensation – serious money in those days. As for the ferrymen who were worried that they would lose business if bridges were built, study the river traffic today and you will see that they were right.

Millbank

The 'mill on the riverbank' was demolished in 1736, but it had previously served Westminster Abbey, on whose property it stood. It was replaced by a mansion built for Sir Robert Grosvenor (one of the Grosvenors of GROSVENOR SQUARE), but goodness knows why he should have wanted to live here – it was in the middle of nowhere and the road was low-lying, muddy and prone to flooding. His descendants obviously thought the same thing: the house was pulled down in 1809 to make way for the Millbank Penitentiary, a building of surpassing gloom much more suited to its surroundings. It was shortly after this that Thomas Cubitt started draining the land and making it fit for non-criminal habitation (see PIMLICO); in the 1850s the CHELSEA Embankment was built, the section between LAMBETH and VAUXHALL bridges being known as Millbank. The embankment originally reached only as far west as the Royal Hospital, but in the 1870s was extended to BATTERSEA Bridge. It covered over the riverside sewer, provided easier road access to Chelsea, encouraged residential development and attracted the prosperous middle classes. So all in all, by the time the penitentiary's useful life came to an end in 1890, the site was much more attractive than it had previously been and it wasn't ridiculous to build an art gallery (see TATE BRITAIN) on it.

Petty France

This means exactly what it looks as if it means – 'little France' – probably because French wool merchants were once centred here. The name is first recorded in the late fifteenth century, long before the French wars of religion encouraged Protestants to leave France *en masse*, so presumably the original merchants' decision to move to WESTMINSTER was a commercial one.

Scotland Yard

A place called Scotland Yard has been the headquarters of the Metropolitan Police ever since that force came into being in 1829. But the name is much older than that. Stow describes 'a large plot of ground inclosed with bricks…called Scotland, where great buildings have been for receipt of the kings of Scotland and other estates of that country'. Specifically Margaret, the sister of Henry VIII, who married a Scottish king (thereby becoming grandmother to Mary, Queen of Scots, and causing a shed-load of trouble), lodged here for a year after she was widowed in 1513, but Scottish kings visiting their English counterparts had been put up at Scotland Yard before that.

The original Great Scotland Yard (there were once also a Middle and a Lower one) is still where it always was, off WHITEHALL. The police moved out in 1890, but took the name with them to various locations before settling in their current headquarters near Victoria Street.

Tate Britain

Sir Henry Tate (1819–99) made a lot of money as a grocer and later as a sugar refiner: not a lot of people know this, but his was the first company in England to produce sugar cubes. After his death his company merged with one called Lyle, and the two names live on on sugar packets to this day.

Henry's name also lives on in a number of art galleries, though he knew only the one now called Tate Britain. Like the patrons of the Courtauld (see SOMERSET HOUSE), he was an art lover and, being grotesquely wealthy, built up a considerable private collection. Towards the end of his life he donated his pictures to the nation and offered a substantial sum to build a gallery to house them, provided the government donated a site. Conveniently, the government had recently demolished MILLBANK Prison and on that site the National Gallery of British Art, as it was originally called, opened in 1897. Known as the Tate Gallery almost from the word go, it became Tate Britain in 2000 to distinguish it from Tate Modern, which opened that year on the other side of the river. The Tate libraries in South London are Henry's legacy too.

Thorney Street

The 'Isle of Thorney' mentioned in the introduction to this section is a tautology – the –ey ending means 'island' and Stow tells us that the area was so-called because it was 'overgrown with thorns and environed with water'; it was created by a number of little branches of the Tyburn (see MARBLE ARCH) flowing into the Thames. The Thames is not as wide at this point as it used to be: Thorney Street is a good 50 metres inland, separated from the river by the sturdy MILLBANK.

Tothill Street

A now obsolete or dialect meaning for 'toot' is 'a lookout place, a hill on which a lookout or beacon is posted', and that is what Tothill was in the thirteenth century. The fields surrounding it – which extended along what is now Victoria Street at least as far as WESTMINSTER Cathedral – were used over the centuries for jousting and tournaments, archery and duelling. They were also, according to the seventeenth-century herbalist Nicholas Culpeper, famous for their parsley.

At that time there were only a few grand houses, inhabited, according to one report, by noblemen and 'the flower of the gentry'. By the early nineteenth century, however, the area had degenerated into what the novelist Georgette Heyer called a back-slum: she describes it as being 'largely composed of wretched hovels, ancient mansions, fallen into depressing decay, and a superfluity of taverns'. There was also, at one time, a prison whose inmates were mostly petty thieves under the age of eighteen. Henry Mayhew, the great Victorian chronicler of London's poor, wrote about one boy who was suspected of throwing stones at a street lamp just so that he would imprisoned (and fed and sheltered) for a month and not have to fend for himself on the streets. The original purpose of the toot that gave Tothill its name had long since been lost, but there was still plenty for the wary citizen to be on the lookout for.

Whitehall

All that remains of the ancient Palace of Whitehall is the Banqueting Hall with its famous Rubens ceiling – the rest burnt down in 1698. The building was originally called York House (it was the residence of Cardinal Wolsey when he was Archbishop of York and was commandeered by Henry VIII after Wolsey fell from grace in 1529) and is not to be confused with the York House mentioned under VILLIERS STREET, where some subsequent Archbishops of York lived.

There are several explanations for the name 'Whitehall': that it was literally a 'white hall', built of light-coloured stone; that it was named by analogy with the (at that time more famous) White Hall in the Palace of Westminster, which later housed the House of Lords; or, as *The London Encyclopaedia* suggests, that it was the custom to call any festive hall a 'white hall'.

Wherever it came from, the name Whitehall was soon applied to the road on which the palace stood. This had existed for centuries, but had previously been known rather cumbersomely as 'the King's Highway from CHARING CROSS to WESTMINSTER'. The metonym 'Whitehall' for 'the government departments based in or near…' dates from the early nineteenth century.

ST JAMES'S

Now here's a thing: one of the most upmarket parts of London takes its name from a leper hospital. Stow tells us that the hospital – dedicated to St James the Less – was 'founded by the citizens of London, before the time of any man's memory, for fourteen sisters, maidens, that were leprous, living chastely and honestly in divine service'. At the time of which he speaks, the hospital would have been well out of town – the traditional place for housing sufferers from this highly infectious disease. It certainly existed during Edward I's reign (1272–1307), because he gave it the right to hold a fair and keep the profits from it. The fair ran for a week (later a fortnight) around St James's Day and was a major event in the calendar of those who wanted to indulge in the lewdness and debauchery that eventually got it banned.

An intriguing footnote here: the fair was suppressed in 1651, under the Puritans. No surprises there: they suppressed anything that sounded as if it might be fun. It was then reinstated after the Restoration of Charles II but banned during his reign. Charles was the most licentious of monarchs – this was the man who employed someone to procure and manage the royal mistresses (see ARLINGTON STREET) – but the St James's Fair was too debauched for him to stomach. The imagination boggles.

I digress. Going back a century or so, at the time of the Dissolution of the Monasteries Henry VIII took over the site of the hospital and built himself a new palace there (he liked palaces – he is said to have owned thirteen within a day's ride of London). He also walled in over 20 hectares of land next to it, the basis of what is today St James's Park; this was later much revamped by Charles II and arranged into something like its current form by John Nash under the auspices of George IV (see REGENT STREET/REGENT'S PARK). St James's Palace didn't become a principal royal residence until 1698, under William and Mary, but by that time the scene was set for the open spaces to the north – known as St James's Field – to be developed into the heartland of expensive hotels, clubs and private residences it is today. The church of St James's PICCADILLY, commissioned by Henry Jermyn (see JERMYN STREET), was a comparative latecomer and took its name from the area rather than the more usual other way round.

Arlington Street

Making money from property was something of a hobby with Charles II's courtiers, though Henry Bennet, Earl of Arlington (1618–85), did it in quite a small way. The king presented him with an area of land in what is now St James's and Henry promptly sold it on to a developer. The street that runs down beside THE RITZ and a smaller street off it commemorate respectively his title and his family name, though Bennett Street is now spelt with two t's.

Henry obviously went in and out of favour at Charles' court. Pepys reports an occasion when there were complaints about the 'bad intelligence' – in the sense of military or political information – that His Majesty was receiving: in particular, it was said, 'the King paid too dear for my Lord Arlington's, in giving him £10,000 and a barony for it'. However, one of Henry's tasks at court was the procuring and managing of the royal mistresses, so presumably he earned his salary keeping these numerous women out of each other's way.

Birdcage Walk

James I (1603–25) built an aviary on the fringes of ST JAMES'S Park and kept exotic birds there. And why not? He also had a menagerie that included camels, crocodiles and an elephant. Hey, he was the king. His grandson Charles II (1660–85) redesigned the park and expanded the aviary (though presumably got rid of the crocodiles); a pair of pelicans presented to him by a Russian ambassador started the tradition of keeping these birds in the park that persists to this day. The aviary seems to have been abandoned by the early eighteenth century, but it had already given its name to a 'walk' alongside the park.

Buckingham Palace

The most casual perusal of this chapter will show that the nobility and gentry were great ones for building grand houses and naming them after themselves. The first Duke of Buckingham and Normanby was no exception: in the early eighteenth century he had a house built on the land previously occupied by Arlington House (see PIMLICO). Shortly after its completion the new Buckingham House was described as 'a graceful palace, very commodiously situated at the westerly end of ST JAMES'S Park, having at one view a prospect of the Mall and other walks, and of the delightful and spacious canal; a seat not to be contemned by the greatest monarch'. Sadly, it didn't stay in the Buckingham family long: the second Duke died of consumption before he was twenty and in 1761 his heir sold the house, rather surprisingly, to the king. The reason was that George III had to spend a lot of time at St James's Palace, where most of the business of the royal court was carried out; being newly married, he wanted to provide his bride with a cosy family home nearby. He wasn't to know just how cosy it would become – Queen Charlotte went on to produce fifteen children, all but two of whom survived into adulthood and two of whom made it to eighty, a truly remarkable statistic for the time.

Anyway, when George IV, the eldest of those fifteen children and a man with rather grander tastes than his father, inherited the family home he didn't think it was up to much. He got his pet architect John Nash (see REGENT STREET/REGENT'S PARK) on the case and spent extortionate sums of public money extending it. So out of hand did the plans and budgets become that George did not live to see the work completed and Buckingham Palace became the monarch's official London residence only in 1837 with the accession of Queen Victoria. It still needed a lot of work to bring it up to the standard normally expected of a royal residence and there is a touch of irony about the fact that much of that work was funded by the sale of George IV's extravagant Pavilion at Brighton.

Interesting that while all this was going on Buckingham Palace had been referred to as the Queen's House and, after Charlotte's death in 1818, as the King's House, but in the longer term nobody seems to have thought of dispensing with the Buckingham connection.

See MARBLE ARCH for more about the problems George IV's grand designs caused.

Constitution Hill

People who care about these things are always banging on about the fact that we don't have a written constitution. So how on earth do we come to have a street called Constitution Hill?

No one seems to know, and the 'best guess' answer – that Charles II took his morning 'constitutionals' here – is, to my mind, disappointingly feeble. However, it gives the chance to repeat an oft-told and almost certainly apocryphal story: that Charles, taking his regular exercise one morning with very few attendants, encountered his brother and heir presumptive, the future James II. James, travelling by coach and well guarded, expressed surprise that the monarch should thus put his life at risk.

'No kind of danger, James,' retorted His Majesty, 'for I am sure no man in England will take away my life to make you King.'

He was more right than he knew: not only did the good people of England wait until Charles was decently in his grave before allowing James to take the throne; they were fed up with him within four years and got rid of him – the only time since the execution of Charles I in 1649 that this has ever happened. There are doubtless those who think deposing an anointed king is unconstitutional, but they should read the first sentence of this entry again.

James, by the way, was Duke of York before he became king, and Duke Street St James's and Duke of York Street, both just off PICCADILLY, are named after him.

Green Park

Lots of trees, lots of grass, very few flowers and no lake: it all adds up to a park being quite green and Green Park is certainly much more monochrome than ST JAMES'S Park, just across the road. According to *The London Encyclopaedia*, the lack of flowers is traditionally attributed to the fact that the park is built over the ground where lepers from the old St James's Hospital were buried. Not a pleasant thought. Let's move on.

Haymarket

'The Market for Hay and Straw, here kept every Tuesday, Thursday, and Saturday, makes [this street] to be of good Account,' says Strype. But don't run away with the idea that it was quiet the rest of the time: there was a market for 'all sorts of cattle' on Mondays and Wednesdays. This all began after the ST JAMES'S Fair, once held near St James's Palace and later in an area near what is now St James's Square, was 'moved on' because it was too lewd and boisterous for the newly moved-in gentry. Haymarket lost no time in becoming as disreputable as its predecessors: in the early nineteenth century 'Haymarket ware' described the lowest sort of prostitute, picked up on the street.

In 1830, the hay market moved out to REGENT'S PARK, but the name was firmly established by then. And see MAYFAIR for more about local residents objecting to rowdy fairs.

Jermyn Street

Henry Jermyn (c.1604–84) was the secretary and favourite of Charles I's queen, Henrietta Maria; he was also a gambler and intriguer with a great enthusiasm for making money. He accompanied the queen into exile in Paris in the early stages of the Civil War and unsubstantiated gossip says that they may have been married after her husband's execution. Either way, he returned to England at the time of the Restoration, was created Earl of St Albans and was granted a lease and later the freehold of a substantial part of St James's Field (see the introduction to this section, page 71). He was largely responsible for the development of the area around St James's Square and commissioned Sir Christopher Wren, the great architect of the day, to build a suitable church. Wren himself described the church as 'beautiful and convenient'; it also has the distinction of being the only Wren church built on a virgin site: the rest of them are restorations or replacements, mainly after the destruction caused by the Great Fire. Although the main entrance to St James's Church is on PICCADILLY, its back door opens on to the street that Henry named after himself.

Naming streets after your patron and his friends and relations was an obvious way of currying favour; and one of Charles II's closest friends was Baptist ('Bab') May (1628–98), said to have been successful at court because he discouraged supplicants from bothering the king about business. After Charles's death he was dismissed – you can see why his name might not have appealed to the staunchly Catholic James II – and sent to be Ranger of Windsor Great Park, a rather nice-sounding position that is held at the time of writing by the Duke of Edinburgh. I mention all this because, should you find yourself in a little lane off Jermyn Street called Babmaes Street and think in passing, 'That's a funny name', this is where it comes from.

Marlborough Road

Running south-ish from PALL MALL to The Mall, this street separates St James's Palace from Marlborough House, designed by Christopher Wren for Sarah Churchill, first Duchess of Marlborough (1660–1744). The friend and confidante of Queen Anne, Sarah was probably the second most powerful person in England during that reign (1702–14). Her husband John commanded the British army and won a famous victory at the Battle of Blenheim in 1704. This inspired the couple to give that name to the second residence they built for themselves – an unobtrusive little palace near Woodstock in Oxfordshire. It also led to Great Marlborough Street near Oxford Circus being named after the duke.

Pall Mall

The Italian *palla a maglio* means 'ball to mallet' and refers to a game similar to croquet. It became very popular in France, where it translated as *palle-maille*. It was played – if you were posh enough – along a tree-lined avenue.

In the 1660s such an avenue existed just to the north of ST JAMES'S Park, but Charles II, an aficionado, had a royal alley built inside the park for the exclusive use of himself and his companions. To do this he re-routed traffic between CHARING CROSS and St James's Palace so that the dust it created would not interfere with the game. The name of the original Pall Mall Alley was eventually reduced to Pall Mall, while the alley inside the park became simply The Mall.

After enthusiasm for the game of pall mall waned, the tree-lined alley of The Mall became a fashionable promenade; by the early eighteenth century the word was being applied to other shaded walks. That it came, from the 1950s, to be adopted by many places that are remarkable for their lack of trees is presumably thanks to some bright marketing person looking for a snappier term than 'pedestrianised shopping precinct'.

Piccadilly

To give an idea of how rural this whole part of town once was, the 1633 edition of Gerard's *Herball*, the first ever catalogue of plants, tells us that 'the small wild buglosse grows upon the drie ditch bankes about Pickadilla'. And who knows? If they ever stop digging up the bus lanes we may find that it makes a comeback.

But that is by the way. It's surprising that one of London's most famous streets should take its name from a joke, but so it seems. A *piccadill* was a wide, decorated collar that was sufficiently popular in the early seventeenth century to make the fortune of a tailor called Robert Baker. When he built himself an impressive house near the Windmill (see WINDMILL STREET) it was promptly dubbed Piccadilly House, presumably by people who thought Rob was getting above himself. The nickname of the house extended to cover the area, and in due course (1819) the 'circus', a name given since the early eighteenth century to a circular area at a road junction.

The easy rhymeability of Piccadilly has made it irresistible to what we might tactfully call the lesser poets. Frederick Locker (1821–95) wrote:

> *Piccadilly! Shops, palaces, bustle and breeze,*
> *The whirring of wheels, and the murmur of trees;*
> *By night or by day, whether noisy or stilly,*
> *Whatever my mood is, I love Piccadilly.*

Stilly?? But it doesn't stop there: in the course of the poem, he works in *shrilly, Lillie, filly, willy-nilly, chilly* and *hilly.* Some years later, James Elroy Flecker (1884–1915), better known for a poem about the golden journey to Samarkand, came up with an elegy for lost love in, of all places, CAMDEN TOWN, which included the verse:

What came of her? The bitter nights
Destroy the rose and lily,
And souls are lost among the lights
Of painted Piccadilly.

It makes you grateful that there are fewer words that rhyme with, say, KNIGHTSBRIDGE or WIMBLEDON Common.

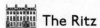 The Ritz

The hotel in Piccadilly is, like its namesake in Paris, named after the Swiss restaurateur and hotelier César Ritz (1850–1918), who founded it after he had been sacked from the SAVOY. Opened in 1906, it was designed to resemble a French château; César employed Auguste Escoffier, one of the most important names in the history of French cookery, as *chef de cuisine* and set about making everything to do with his hotel as luxurious as it could be. Which is where the adjective *ritzy* comes from. Although it has been suggested that the modern word *scoff* derives from Escoffier, there is no etymological justification for this and the great man, who took his cuisine seriously, would have been deeply offended at anyone who dared to scoff – or scoff at – his food.

Vigo Street

Very few people nowadays could give you the dates of the War of the Spanish Succession (1701–14, since you ask) nor tell you more about it than is clear from its name. Yet Britain was deeply involved in it and won an important victory at Blenheim (see MARLBOROUGH ROAD) and another at Vigo Bay, hence the name of this street. Vigo at least is in

Spain; Blenheim is in Bavaria. Explaining why the British were fighting the French in Germany over who was to rule Spain is, happily, beyond the scope of this book.

BELGRAVIA AND BEYOND

The village of Belgrave just outside Chester is now so small that it isn't marked on a standard road atlas, but it gave its name to this well-appointed part of London. Why? Well, it is within the grounds of the Duke of Westminster's country estate, Eaton Hall, adjacent to the village of Eccleston. As well as owning substantial chunks of Cheshire, the Duke of Westminster was and is the landlord of large swathes of London SW1. The present Duke's holdings, worth an estimated $13 billion, make him the UK's wealthiest landowner and earn him fifty-seventh place in *Forbes* magazine's list of the world's billionaires. In addition to the area known as Belgravia, Belgrave Square, Eaton Square and Eccleston Square and various roads, mews and crescents in their vicinity all take their names from the Duke's Cheshire possessions and all form part of the Grosvenor estate, Grosvenor being the Duke's family name (see also GROSVENOR SQUARE). For the meanings of the names themselves, see BELGRAVE SQUARE, below.

In fact, at the time of the development the head of the family was a mere Marquess: Robert Grosvenor (1767–1845) was the first of three men to bear the title Marquess of Westminster before it was upgraded to Duke in 1874. It was he who felt the family needed a smart town house and built the mansion on PARK LANE where the Grosvenor House Hotel now stands.

In case you were wondering, the Queen's private fortune isn't in the same ballpark as the Duke of Westminster's – you can measure it in mere millions. Most of her stuff (which does run into billions) is held in trust for the nation, which is nice for us but means it doesn't count in *Forbes*'s list.

Belgrave Square

Following on from the list of the Duke of Westminster's possessions given above, *Belgrave* comes from the Old French for 'beautiful wood'; you could argue that it should really be 'Belgrove', but these things have always tended to get muddled over the centuries. *Eaton* is composed of two very common Old English elements and means 'farmstead or estate on a river': it occurs again and again around the country, in Nuneaton, Long Eaton and many more. *Eccleston* is also a 'farmstead or estate' and would originally have belonged to a church, *Eccles–* being derived from the Latin *ecclesia* and associated with the French *église*.

Ebury Square/Ebury Street

The *–bury* ending here is the same as in BLOOMSBURY and means a manor, in this case a manor on a piece of dry ground in a marsh (for more about the dampness of the area, see PIMLICO). Ebury existed, as Eia, at the time of the Domesday Book, when it belonged to a Norman noble called Geoffrey de Mandeville. Geoffrey gave it – probably for the good of his soul, possibly in exchange for hard cash – to the Abbot and Convent of WESTMINSTER. It remained in their possession until the time of Henry VIII, when so much land that belonged to the Church suddenly found its way into the hands of the Crown. During the reign of Elizabeth I (1558–1603) what is now Ebury Square formed part of a farm of about 166 hectares which was sublet to 'divers persons, who, for their private commodity, did inclose the same, and had made pastures of arable land; thereby not only annoying Her Majesty in her walks and passages, but to the hindrance of her game'. A less devoted royalist than Strype, who reported this information, might have written 'so that they could grow things to eat' in place of 'for their private commodity', but no – the Queen's annoyance was what mattered.

Like many ancient names, Ebury stuck around after the area was developed from the eighteenth century onwards.

Knightsbridge

This is an Old English name that pre-dates the Domesday Book, but allowing for minor developments of meaning it still does what it says on the tin. No problem about the bridge bit: it was at the point where the main road west crossed the old river known as the West Bourne (see WESTBOURNE GROVE/WESTBOURNE PARK), about midway between the present HYDE PARK Corner and Knightsbridge tube stations. The knights, on the other hand, have evolved: in those early days the word meant simply 'boy' or 'lad', particularly one employed as a retainer. One explanation for the name Knightsbridge is that it was a place where the local yoof hung out.

Knightsbridge is recorded as a separate town in the reign of Edward III (1327–77), though it would have been little more than a hamlet. Stow tells us that there was a lazar house (for the housing of lepers, which was always done at a safe distance from more populous areas – see ST JAMES'S) here at about that time, and also that during the reign of Edward's grandson and successor Richard II (1377–99) 'motion was made that no Butcher should kill no flesh within London, but at Knightsbridge, or such like distance of place from the walls of the city'. As late as the eighteenth century, Knightsbridge remained sufficiently separated from London for 'footpads' (highwaymen on foot) to operate here, robbing the Bristol-bound mail coach with impunity on a quiet road that ran spitting distance from where Harrod's now stands.

Pimlico

The experts seem to agree that in the late sixteenth century a publican called Ben Pimlico had an inn in Hoxton (see DALSTON). A guide to Pimlico sold in the local shops tells us that he kept a fine 'nut browne' ale which acquired fame throughout London and that 'the name was copied for a pub near the present Victoria Station, where Pimlico [meaning the district, not the man] was recorded by 1626'. If this is true – and it probably is – then it simply means that, thanks to Ben's nut browne, 'Pimlico' was deemed a good name for a pub. Whether Ben was starting a franchise or someone else was cashing in on his fame is not recorded. The name of the inn duly extended to the area around it, as it did in ANGEL and White Hart Lane (see the box *The Round Ball and the Oval Ball*, page 240).

It may have had an inn in 1626, but as late as 1687 Pimlico is described as having only four houses, though they were grand ones. One was Arlington House, home of the Earl of Arlington mentioned under ARLINGTON STREET, on part of the site of the present BUCKING-HAM PALACE. The area that most people now call Pimlico wasn't built up until the nineteenth century, for the simple reason that it was at best marshy and at worst simply under water. In 1834 it was still famous for its osier beds, osiers being a form of willow with flexible branches for making baskets, fencing and other useful things, and the willow being a tree that likes damp conditions. There is still a Willow Walk tucked away in the back streets behind WESTMINSTER Cathedral.

Then along came an enterprising builder-developer called Thomas Cubitt (1788–1855). Deciding that there was money to be made out of developing an area so close to Westminster, he set about raising the level of the ground in Pimlico, using, among other things, tonnes and tonnes of dry soil from the recently dug-out ST KATHARINE'S DOCK near the Tower.

But where did the name Pimlico come from in the first place? Well, scholarly opinion suggests that it may derive from the name of a Native American tribe discovered when Sir Walter Raleigh founded a colony in Virginia in the 1580s. This colony was famously disastrous and a number of the settlers promptly abandoned it. Had one of them somehow acquired 'Pimlico' as a nickname and brought it home with them? And if so, was it Ben's dad? Or even Ben himself? Who knows? It's a thought to be discussed at leisure, perhaps over a pint or two of nut browne.

Wilton Crescent/Wilton Place/Wilton Road

This name crops up so frequently in KNIGHTSBRIDGE, BELGRAVIA and PIMLICO that you might assume that Mr Wilton was a major landowner or at least related to one. And you would be right. Except that he wasn't a Mr, he was the first Earl of Wilton and father-in-law of Robert Grosvenor, the first Marquess of Westminster, who owned the land hereabouts when it was developed into Belgravia.

WESTMINSTER CENTRAL

A varied area, stretching from HYDE PARK in the west to the borders of the City in the east, encompassing some of London's most expensive real estate and what in the past were some of its worst slums. Red-light areas and elegant city squares, great philanthropists and dodgy vicars - all human life is here.

FROM COVENT GARDEN TO THE RIVER

Covent Garden is a corruption of 'Convent Garden': the whole area was once a garden belonging to WESTMINSTER Abbey. The monks grew and ate apples, plums and pears, as well as cultivating barley for brewing purposes. The area began to take on the form we now know from the sixteenth century, when Edward VI (1547–53) granted it to John Russell, first Earl of Bedford (c. 1485–1555); the name is recorded as 'Covent' in 1570. Development of Covent Garden as London's first square was begun in the time of the fourth Earl, Francis Russell (1593–1641), who was lucky enough to have as his architect the great Inigo Jones (1573–1652). The square itself was known as 'the Piazza' from its inception; Inigo had trained in Italy, so the Italian name was probably his idea.

It was Francis Russell who obtained a licence to set up a fruit and vegetable market along the wall of Bedford House, to the south side of the square, and there fresh produce was sold from 1670 till the market moved south of the river in 1974. A hundred years later the Russell family could afford to move out of what was by then a bustling area and names connected with them crop up again in the section on BLOOMSBURY.

The border of the City of Westminster does a strange kink through Covent Garden, so some of the streets included here are officially in the borough of CAMDEN; however, it seems sensible to put all the area generally thought of as Covent Garden in one section, with apologies to Camden for encroaching on its territory.

Aldwych

Although the crescent known as Aldwych dates from only 1905, the name is Old English and means 'old trading place'. It refers to the important Saxon settlement of Lundenwīc that grew up outside the walls in the seventh to ninth centuries (see the Introduction, page 3). The City's fortunes revived after Alfred the Great defeated the Danes in 886 and Lundenwīc was in turn neglected until London's population grew sufficiently to start overflowing the walls again. 'Aldwych' as a name for this part of town dates from the late fourteenth century, by which time the former trading place was indeed old.

Bedfordbury

This is an odd name for a street that has no claims to being fortified or part of a manor, which is what the ending –*bury* normally means (see, for example, ALDERMANBURY and BLOOMSBURY). The Bedford connection is obvious (see the introduction to this section), but the best guess for *–bury* is that it is a nineteenth-century joke, based on the fact that 'fortified' was a euphemism for drunk. In the days when much of Covent Garden was a slum, Bedfordbury was one of the worst parts of it: George Sala, writing in the 1850s, describes…

> *…a devious, slimy little reptile of a place, whose tumble-down tenements and reeking courts spume forth plumps of animated rags, such as can be equalled in no London thoroughfare. I don't think there are five windows in Bedfordbury with a whole pane of glass in them.*

There's much more in this vein, but you get the picture. Anyway, along this little street there were no fewer than six pubs. The suggestion is that *–bury* was adopted into the street name because so many of its inhabitants were permanently…fortified.

Bow Street

According to Strype, Bow Street was so-called because it ran in the shape of a bent bow. He also tells us that it was 'well inhabited' – his expression for 'posh people lived there' (see LEICESTER SQUARE). Within fifteen years of his book being published, however, this was no longer the case: the Covent Garden Theatre, on the site of what is now the Royal Opera House, opened in 1732 and very soon lowered the tone. At a time when female performers habitually wore masks, wigs, hooped skirts, panniers and high heels, a dancer named Marie Sallé broke with tradition by discarding her corset and putting on Greek robes to appear in her ballet version of *Pygmalion*.

This Bow Street is the one that appears on the classic Monopoly board. The connection between the three orange properties is police stations: the one in Bow Street opened in 1749 and became famous for the band of constables (founded by Henry Fielding, author of *Tom*

Jones) known as the Bow Street Runners. As for the others, for Marlborough Street, see MARLBOROUGH ROAD. Vine Street, just off REGENT STREET, is adjacent to a former vineyard. Wikipedia gives the dire warning that, if you are doing a Monopoly pub crawl, having a drink in every property on the board, you will come unstuck on Vine Street because there are no licensed premises. As a matter of passing interest, none of the three police stations is still in use. And see BOW LANE for other forms of curvature that gave rise to place names.

Charing Cross

Charing comes from the Old English for a bend in a road or river; the Thames takes a sharp bend at this point and the old main road that ran from WESTMINSTER to the City roughly followed it (imagine coming up WHITEHALL from Parliament Square and turning right into the STRAND and you won't be far wrong). The cross is one of the twelve so-called 'Eleanor Crosses' erected by Edward I in honour of his late wife. Queen Eleanor died near Lincoln in 1290 and her body was carried back to London; a cross marked each of the places where her body rested in the course of her twelve-day journey. The last of these was originally at the top of modern Whitehall (a plaque just behind the statue of Charles I on TRAFALGAR SQUARE marks the spot) and became the point from which distances to and from London were measured. In 1647 – a time when memorials to royalty were not the height of fashion – Parliament decreed that it should be pulled down; the one that now stands outside Charing Cross Station is a Victorian replica.

Cockspur Street

Cock-fighting was a popular sport in Georgian times and there was a cockpit for the purpose in WHITEHALL. Fighting cocks wore spurs, the better to wound each other, and the spurs were presumably sold in this street, conveniently close at hand. There may also be a connection with the nearby Cock Tavern, which was, according to Pepys, 'famous for good meat, and particularly pease-porridge'.

Somebody else connected with wearing spurs was Henry Percy, son of the Duke of Northumberland, a hot-headed rebel nicknamed Hotspur. Although a historical character, Hotspur is best known from his appearance in Shakespeare's *Henry IV*, and the implication – unsubstantiated but plausible – is that he made good use of his spurs while riding flat out wherever he was going. Coincidentally, his family owned a lot of land in north-east London and the football team Tottenham Hotspur is said to have named itself after the Percys' most famous son (see also White Hart Lane in the box *The Round Ball and the Oval Ball*, page 240).

Denmark Street

London's Tin Pan Alley has been associated with music since long before the Rolling Stones recorded their first album here: the nickname dates from the 1920s and it had been known as the place to go for sheet music for several decades before that. But the street was built in the 1680s and the name probably honours Queen Anne's consort George of Denmark, who had married the then princess in 1683 and is also remembered in DENMARK HILL.

Drury Lane

This early centre of theatreland has a disappointingly prosaic name – it comes from a family called Drury who had a mansion here in the sixteenth century. The street had been there long before that, however, and was once known rather grandly as the Via de ALDWYCH. During the reign of James I it was briefly called Prince's Street, but for some reason this didn't catch on. Then after the Restoration the name of the street became inextricably linked with its theatre and with theatre in general: between 1682 and 1714 the Theatre Royal Drury Lane was the only licensed playhouse in London and no further attempt to change its name would have stood a chance.

Floral Street

This narrow street runs alongside the site of the old Floral Hall, now part of the refurbished Royal Opera House. The Floral Hall was big business from about the 1830s, when middle-class Londoners discovered the charms of flowers for decoration. From Covent Garden flowers were sold to retailers throughout the city.

Nearby Rose Street seems to have got its name a different way. Strype refers to this as White Rose Street; it pre-dates the flower market by at least 100 years and was probably named after a pub.

Garrick Street

David Garrick (1717–79) was the great tragic actor of his day. He lived for many years in Southampton Street, conveniently situated for the Theatre Royal DRURY LANE, where he was star, manager and co-owner. A generation later, his mantle was assumed by John Kemble (1757–1823), who also has a street nearby named after him. Round the corner from Kemble Street is Kean Street, named after another actor, Edmund Kean (c.1789–1833) but, surprisingly and sexistly, there is no such remembrance of Kemble's sister, the great tragedienne Sarah Siddons (1755–1831).

In fact it is not Garrick Street that is named after David Garrick, but the Garrick Club, a gentlemen's club, many of whose members are actors. Its headquarters were originally in King Street; it moved to its present building in 1864 and only then did Garrick Street acquire its name – making it not 'David Garrick Street' so much as 'the street where the Garrick Club is'.

Great Queen Street

Named after Anne of Denmark, consort of James I (1603–25), who is also the 'queen' of the Queen's House at GREENWICH. When Great Queen Street was built this was rather an isolated area, but the street was part of the route between WHITEHALL Palace and Theobald's Road, the importance of which is explained in that entry.

Henrietta Street

So called in honour of Henrietta Maria, Charles I's queen, who was on the throne at the time COVENT GARDEN was laid out. Other 'royal' streets in the area include King Street, James Street (after the recently deceased James I) and the now vanished Charles Street and York Street (Charles I, his parents' second son, had been known as the Duke of York until his brother's premature death). To the east of the Piazza, Catherine Street was built a few decades later and named after Charles II's queen, Catherine of Braganza, who, being Portuguese, is also remembered in Portugal Street, on the other side of Kingsway (see the box *Which King, Which Queen?*, page 155).

Long Acre

In Henry VIII's day this was a 'great field' called The Elms, with a road called Long Acar (as Stow spells it) running through it. The old sense of 'acre' is the one involved here: it is an area of ploughed land, rather than a specific measurement. Stow gives us the edifying information that the name The Elms was in place 'when Mortimer was executed and let hang two days and two nights to be seene of the people'. By Mortimer he almost certainly means Roger, the first Earl of March (1287–1330) who, as the lover of Edward II's wife Isabella, was allegedly involved with her in a plot to depose the king and was hanged, drawn and quartered for his pains. Roger has the distinction of having been the first person to be executed at Tyburn (see MARBLE ARCH).

Maiden Lane

This thoroughfare, which ran across the old 'convent garden', pre-dates Inigo Jones's development and may have a rather less dignified name than some of its neighbours: it could derive from *midden*, an old word for dung heap. For those looking for something higher minded, there is a much-repeated but strangely unsubstantiated report that a statue of the Virgin Mary 'adorned the corner of the street in Catholic days'. The source of this story is normally cited as Isaac D'Israeli, father of the nineteenth-century Prime Minister, but he was quoting an earlier account and it is unlikely that this is the explanation of the name. In Stow's time there was another Maiden Lane further east, which he records as also known as Engain Lane, but no one seems to be sure what this means either, so that is no help. We probably need to accept that the monks of Westminster needed heaps of organic fertiliser to put on their productive garden, and that they had to keep it somewhere…

Monmouth Street

It is tempting to say that this was named after Charles II's illegitimate son the Duke of Monmouth – tempting because he was to some a glamorous figure and because he is the only Monmouth most of us have heard of. (In case you haven't, he was the perpetrator of the so-called

Monmouth Rebellion of 1685, in which, as a Protestant, he attempted to put himself on the throne in place of his recently deceased father's Catholic brother James II.) However, the dates don't really fit and it is more likely that the street honours an earlier and less scandalous Earl of Monmouth, a diplomat and favourite at the courts of both James I and Charles I. Confusingly, on early maps Monmouth Street is the name given to part of what is now SHAFTESBURY AVENUE; it disappeared when that thoroughfare was built in the 1870s and re-emerged in its present location in the 1930s.

It would, however, be a shame to pass over the opportunity to tell a few gory stories about the glamorous Duke of Monmouth. After his failed rebellion he was condemned to death by execution and on mounting the scaffold asked the executioner, the highly experienced Jack Ketch, not to make a botch of the job: Ketch had recently taken four blows to despatch Lord Russell. Ketch was so thrown by this remark that he did indeed make a botch of it. The historian Lord Macaulay takes up the tale:

The first blow inflicted only a slight wound. The Duke struggled, rose from the block, and looked reproachfully at the executioner. The head sank down once more. The stroke was repeated again and again; but still the neck was not severed, and the body continued to move. Yells of rage and horror rose from the crowd. Ketch flung down the axe with a curse. 'I cannot do it,' he said; 'my heart fails me.' 'Take up the axe, man,' cried the sheriff. 'Fling him over the rails,' roared the mob. At length the axe was taken up. Two more blows extinguished the last remains of life; but a knife was used to separate the head from the shoulders. The crowd was wrought up to such an ecstasy of rage that the executioner was in danger of being torn in pieces, and was conveyed away under a strong guard.

There are those who believe that the entire execution was faked and that Monmouth escaped to France to become the Man in the Iron Mask: or that the execution was real but that the head was balanced back on the neck so that the victim could sit for a posthumous portrait. The portrait said to have inspired this tale is in the National Portrait Gallery in London, but their website now describes it as a portrait of an unknown man, with several cogent reasons why it couldn't be Monmouth. Legend persists, though, as legends do.

Neal Street

Thomas Neale (1641–99), after whom (despite the spelling) this street is named, was what nowadays would be called an entrepreneur, or perhaps a multi-tasker. Holding various positions in the households of Charles II and later William III, he had the right to license or close down gaming houses and, according to John Evelyn, introduced a lottery 'in imitation of those in Venice'. He was also responsible for the first official postal service in the North American colonies, and in England was involved in establishing an early version of a national bank. For the last twenty years of his life he was Master of the Mint, a post in which he was succeeded, strangely enough, by Isaac Newton (now *there* was a multi-tasker for you). In amongst all this, Thomas took it upon himself to develop part of the slum near ST GILES into the area that is now SEVEN DIALS. He obviously spread his talents too thinly – despite all the above, he managed to die penniless.

Northumberland Avenue

Although it is now named after the Earls (and later Dukes) of Northumberland, the great house that once sat on this site was built in the early seventeenth century as the pied à terre of the Earl of

Northampton. When I say pied à terre, I should add that the frontage was 50 metres long and the court which looked out over the river was 25 metres square, making it quite a sizeable second home.

Through a complicated chain of inheritance Northampton House went through a period of being Suffolk House before passing into the hands of the Northumberlands who, a couple of centuries earlier, had been the most powerful family in the north of England. (Their most famous son was Henry Hotspur of Shakespeare's *Henry IV* – see COCK-SPUR STREET.) To add to the confusion, in 1682 the Northumberland heiress married the Duke of Somerset, whose ancestors had already named a grand house not 500 metres away (see SOMERSET HOUSE). As a result, the Duke and Duchess of Somerset lived in grand style in a house they continued to call Northumberland House.

The house was, perhaps, too grand for its own good: the coping along the side that faced on to the STRAND was 'a border of capital letters' and at the time of the funeral of Anne of Denmark, James I's queen, in 1619, the letter S was pushed off by 'the incautious leaning forward of sightseers on the roof', killing an unfortunate young man in the crowd below.

Development took its toll in the end: in 1873 Northumberland House was demolished to allow a new road, Northumberland Avenue, to connect the recently built thoroughfare of the VICTORIA EMBANK-MENT to TRAFALGAR SQUARE.

St Clement Danes

Although this is now perhaps best known for its links with the Royal Air Force, there has been a church on the site since at least the eleventh century. Its long-ago connection with the Danes is the subject of debate; some say that an earlier (ninth-century) church was founded by Danes who, after being defeated by Alfred the Great, were allowed to settle outside the City walls. To add weight to this explanation, Stow tells us about the first King Harold, who died in 1040: he was an illegitimate son of Canute and thus of Danish descent. He was buried in WESTMINSTER Abbey, but Harthacnut, Canute's legitimate son, had him dug up and thrown into the Thames 'in revenge of a displeasure done to his mother'. A fisherman rescued the body and caused it to be interred at St Clement's, where, according to Stow, other Danes were also buried. The churchyard has long since disappeared under newer buildings, so it's impossible to check this one out, but see LAMBETH for the tale of Harthacnut's comeuppance.

Only one other London church, St Clement, Eastcheap, in the City, is dedicated to St Clement, who was an early Bishop of Rome. Both claim to be the original of 'Oranges and lemons say the bells of St Clement's', and there is no hard evidence to enable us to decide between them.

St Giles

Giles is regarded as the patron saint of beggars, cripples, lepers and other outcasts; all over medieval Europe churches dedicated to him tended to be outside the city walls, because beggars and cripples were not permitted to go through the gates (see Cripplegate in the box *The City Gates*, page 37). Given that, as the crow flies, the part of London still known as St Giles in the Fields is a good 2 kilometres outside the old City walls, it was an excellent place to build a leper hospital with church attached in the early years of the twelfth century. Also, of course, it was surrounded by fields, and remained so for several hundred years thereafter: in 1665 it was still sufficiently distant from the centre of civilisation for thousands of plague victims to be buried in its churchyard.

As London expanded westwards, new developments tended to be upmarket – it was the rich who could afford to move out of the crowded medieval City and buy or build larger houses with more land attached. St Giles had its fifteen minutes of prosperity, but not much more than that: by the mid-seventeenth century it was overpopulated and degenerate. Dickens, describing in *A Tale of Two Cities* (1859) the general lawlessness of London, observes that...

> *...musketeers went into St. Giles's, to search for contraband goods, and the mob fired on the musketeers, and the musketeers fired on the mob, and nobody thought any of these occurrences much out of the common way.*

The term 'rookery', from the way rooks cluster together in large numbers when roosting, was widely used in the nineteenth century to describe a slum, but the one round St Giles was probably the first. See also SEVEN DIALS.

The Savoy

The first building we know of on this site is the Savoy Palace, built in the thirteenth century by Peter, Count of Savoy, who had come to England with his niece Eleanor of Provence when she married Henry III (1216–72). Savoy was at that time an independent county occupying the bottom right-hand corner of France and the top left of Italy, with bits of Switzerland and Monaco thrown in.

The palace was burnt down during the Peasants' Revolt of 1381 and subsequently rebuilt as a hospital for the poor; it then languished for a couple of hundred years until the site was bought by the theatre impresario Richard d'Oyly Carte in 1880. He wanted a theatre dedicated to the production of Gilbert and Sullivan operas and built what he called the Savoy Theatre for the purpose. Profits from this venture enabled him to fulfil his dream of building a luxury hotel next door.

Seven Dials

The streets around this now trendy shopping area were once part of the most disreputable slum in London, depicted in Hogarth's *Gin Lane* and described under ST GILES, above. The fact that Hogarth's work dates from just sixty years after Thomas Neale of NEAL STREET fame had spent a fortune attempting to pull the area out of the gutter gives an idea of what a spectacular failure his development had been. But it started out in 1691 as a grand plan, with six streets radiating out from a central 'circus' in which stood a column decorated with six sundials. A seventh street, the eastern part of what is now Mercer Street (named after the Worshipful Company of Mercers, who owned the land and licensed the building work), had been added by the early years of the eighteenth century, in time to give the place its name but too late for anyone to alter the column to match.

There is a strange story attached to that column, though. It was taken down in 1773 after word got around that there was buried treasure beneath it (goodness knows why – it certainly wasn't true). After lying idle for some decades, it was bought by the good people of Weybridge and erected on their village green in honour of Frederica, Duchess of York (1767–1820). She had been married to one of the numerous unlovable sons of George III (called Frederick, oddly enough) and had lived nearby for many years after separating from her husband. The original column is still in Weybridge; the modern replica at Seven Dials itself dates only from 1989, when COVENT GARDEN was being revitalised. It was the first monumental column to be erected in London since Nelson's Column in TRAFALGAR SQUARE in the 1840s.

Shaftesbury Avenue

As the entries for SEVEN DIALS and ST GILES show, this area was for a long time one of the grottiest parts of town; knocking down the slums, rebuilding better houses and putting a major road through the lot was widely acclaimed as a thoroughly good thing. It is fitting that the new road should have been named in honour of the great philanthropist the seventh Earl of Shaftesbury (1801–85), who had died only months before it was officially opened: much of his philanthropy had been concerned with the relief of the poor hereabouts. Lord Shaftesbury is also commemorated in the statue in PICCADILLY Circus generally referred to as Eros. In fact it is a sculpture of Eros's brother Anteros, who celebrates requited, mutual love and is therefore a much better representation of philanthropy than the god who made mischief by shooting arrows into his hapless victims and causing them to fall in love with the wrong people.

Somerset House

As mentioned in passing under NORTHUMBERLAND AVENUE, Somerset House was the mansion – some would say palace – of the Duke of Somerset, begun in 1547. This was the year that Edward VI came to the throne. The Duke – Edward Seymour in private life – was the nine-year-old king's uncle and became Lord Protector of England, the most powerful man in the country. So he deserved a splendid house.

Much good it did him: he overstepped himself and had his head cut off before the house was finished. The king, a great diary-keeper, recorded the charges against his uncle as 'ambition, vainglory, entering into rash wars in mine youth, negligent looking on Newhaven, enriching himself of my treasure, following his own opinion, and doing all by his own authority, etc.' Newhaven meant Ambleteuse, one of

England's last remaining possessions in France, lost in 1549. More intriguing, I feel, is the 'etc.' – after a list such as this, what *else* could the poor devil have done?

This part of town – along what is now the STRAND – was very popular for opulent non-royal residences: the former homes of the Dukes of Arundel and Essex are remembered in nearby street names. Essex House must have seen some fun in its time, because it was owned first by Elizabeth I's favourite the Earl of Leicester, and after his death by the Earl of Essex, whose name was also linked with the queen's. See also THE SAVOY.

Art lovers may know Somerset House principally as the home of the Courtauld Gallery. This is named after its founder and chief bene-factor, Samuel Courtauld (1876–1947), the great-nephew of the earlier Samuel Courtauld who made his fortune from inventing rayon. The name is originally French; Sam and Sam's ancestors were Huguenot refugees.

Strand

This is 'strand' in the old-fashioned poetic sense of the shore beside sea, lake or, in this case, river. Until the Thames was widened and the VICTORIA EMBANKMENT built, the Strand was appreciably nearer the river than it is now.

Trafalgar Square

It's difficult to imagine at this distance – over 200 years – just how much Napoleon rampaging around Europe horrified the British and therefore just what a popular hero Vice-Admiral Lord (Horatio) Nelson was. He won resounding victories at the Battles of the Nile and Copenhagen, but his crowning glory was the battle in which he lost his life, off Cape Trafalgar in south-western Spain in 1805. He was awarded a state funeral, only the second non-royal to be given this honour (the first was the Elizabethan soldier-poet Philip Sidney); there have been only seven since – a handful of prime ministers and soldiers (Wellington, Churchill, people like that) and Charles Darwin.

The square named after his last battle was laid out in the 1830s and Nelson's Column erected in the 1840s. At great expense, apparently: the square's granite work alone is said to have cost upwards of £10,000 – much the same as the annual income of Mr Darcy in *Pride and Prejudice*, which made him a very rich man – and the column not much less. But many visitors and even more pigeons have enjoyed it ever since, so let us not be stingy about it.

Victoria Embankment

Anyone interested in the way the Thames has been managed over the centuries should stroll into Embankment Gardens and have a look at the York Watergate. It used to give access to York House from the river (see VILLIERS STREET): now it is simply a pretty thing sitting rather meaninglessly in a park.

The reason for this is that in the 1860s some 14 hectares of land were reclaimed from the bend in the Thames here: the river became about 140 metres narrower and the road now called the Victoria Embankment was built. (The lesser-known Albert Embankment runs along the south side of the river, between VAUXHALL and LAMBETH bridges, and dates from about the same time.) A traffic-calming measure *par excellence*, the project had first been proposed by Wren after the Great Fire but was not brought to fruition until 200 years later. Delays in planning permission, one would guess.

The new road was shored up by a granite wall some 2.5 metres thick, with foundations sunk up to 9 metres below the low-water mark.

Wheatley, waxing eloquent about this magnificent feat of engineering that had been completed in his lifetime, tells us that the reclaimed land had formerly at low tide been a 'pestiferous slime'. So its drying up would have done a few Dickensian characters out of their livelihood, but was considered a good thing by the middle and upper classes.

Londoners generally refer to this road as 'the Embankment' – goodness knows, Queen Victoria gets enough mentions elsewhere; like MONUMENT and BANK the tube station doesn't have a definite article.

Villiers Street

This busy little street running up from Embankment station to the STRAND takes its name from George Villiers, second Duke of Buckingham (1628–87). George's father, also George, the first Duke, had been a 'favourite', to use a courtly euphemism, of James I, a position that had given him the money to acquire the splendid York House on the Strand, the former home of the Archbishops of York.

The second duke sold the house to developers in 1672, making it a condition of the sale that each and every aspect of his name and title be recorded in the new streets. So not only were there to be a George Street, a Villiers Street, a Duke Street and a Buckingham Street; he also insisted on an Of Alley. Some killjoy, completely missing the point, has changed three of these names: Of Alley is now York Place; Duke Street is John Adam Street, after the eighteenth-century architect who, with his brother Robert, designed a number of buildings here; and, although there is still a George Court, George Street has been rechristened York Buildings. So Villiers Street and Buckingham Street are all that remain to remind us of the overpowering ego (or subversive sense of humour) of George Villiers, second Duke Of Buckingham.

MAYFAIR

Public fairs used to be big business and May Day (I May) was an important holiday, heralding the beginning of summer. Put the two together and you have a full two weeks of celebration. From 1686 to 1764 London's great May Fair was held in the district that now bears its name. At the start of its career, the May Fair was on the very outskirts of town; as we shall see in the course of this section the ensuing century saw a huge amount of development. The great and the good, or at least the titled and self-important, moved in and were soon objecting to the 'yearly riotous and tumultuous assembly', which they considered 'a public nuisance and inconvenience'. *Tatler* in 1709 reported that 'May Fair is utterly abolished, and we hear that Mr Pinkethman has removed his ingenious company of strollers to GREENWICH'. It is to be hoped that the people of Greenwich were less stuffy and more appreciative than those of Mayfair. In fact *Tatler*'s announcement was premature – the fair was allowed to resume a few years later, but local objections continued and in 1764 it was officially transferred to the HAYMARKET. Not very far away, but far enough to placate the people living in what was now very much the smart end of town.

Albemarle Street

As we saw in the section on ST JAMES'S, Charles II handed out a lot of prime real estate to his loyal courtiers (doubtless with a certain amount of money or favours changing hands), and most of them took the opportunity to build themselves ostentatious mansions. One such was Edward Hyde, Earl of Clarendon (1609–74), Lord Chancellor in the early years of Charles's reign. He spent the phenomenal sum of over

£40,000 on what John Evelyn described as 'without hyperbole the best contrived, the most useful, graceful and magnificent house in England'. Interesting that the great diarist didn't understand the meaning of hyperbole, but let that pass.

Unfortunately, Clarendon had to go into exile to escape a charge of treason and his son, badly in debt, sold the mansion – for rather less than it had cost to build – to Christopher Monck, the second Duke of Albemarle, who promptly changed its name to his own. This man's father, the first Duke, was George Monck, the politician and soldier who played a starring role in the Restoration of Charles II. His son seems not to have been of the same mettle – Evelyn (who lived in DOVER STREET and was on chummy terms with most of the local grandees) refers to 'the prodigious waste [he] had made of his estate since the old man died'. Doubtless to fend off his creditors, Christopher sold Albemarle House to a consortium headed by a financier called Sir Thomas Bond (see BOND STREET), who demolished it to make way for new development. Part of the development was modern Albemarle Street, named in honour of the house it had replaced.

The Earl of Clarendon has no such memorial in MAYFAIR (hardly surprising, given that he was living abroad in disgrace). However, his daughter, Anne Hyde, married the future James II and two of the daughters of that marriage – Mary II and Anne – became queen in their own right. So Clarendon, as grandfather to two English queens, has a claim to fame equalled only by Henry VII, grandfather of Mary I and Elizabeth I. Not bad for someone who was impeached by the House of Commons and was, by all accounts, a thoroughly unpleasant man.

HYDE PARK, by the way, has nothing to do with this family.

Berkeley Square

Lord Berkeley of Stratton (1602–78), a friend of the Earl of Clarendon (see ALBEMARLE STREET), acquired a parcel of Clarendon's estate from him and built on it a mansion about which John Evelyn had mixed feelings: 'It was very well built, and has many noble rooms, but they are not very convenient…they are all rooms of state, without closets.' In other words, there was nowhere where the family could relax and put their feet up – he doesn't mean that there wasn't any cupboard space. The highlight, according to Evelyn, was the garden, which he described as 'incomparable thanks to the "inequality" [that is, the undulating nature] of the ground'. Later bought by the Duke of Devonshire and renamed Devonshire House, the mansion burned down in 1733, but Berkeley Square, Berkeley Street and Stratton Street all owe their names to the original owner. And, as testament to the area's one-time ruralness and continuing hilliness, there are still a Farm Street, a Hill Street and a Hay Hill nearby.

Bond Street

A Victorian handbook of London refers to 'Sir Thomas Bond, of PECKHAM, in the County of Surrey', which may come as a surprise to anyone who has visited Peckham recently. Sir Thomas (1620–85) was Comptroller of the Household to the Queen Mother – Henrietta Maria, widow of Charles I and mother of Charles II – and also a speculator and developer. The land that came with his purchase of Albemarle House (see ALBEMARLE STREET) covered over 9 hectares and from 1680 he and his associates were primarily responsible for the development of what are now Old Bond Street, ALBEMARLE STREET and DOVER STREET, running north from PICCADILLY through this estate.

New Bond Street, a northern extension of the older part, came into existence during a second phase of development, in the 1720s, but the established residents would have nothing to do with it. It was they who insisted on the 'newness' (which obviously equated with 'upstart', in their view) being conveyed in the name. In fact, this attitude persisted at least into the 1920s, when Westminster City Council suggested dropping the 'Old' and the 'New' and calling the entire street simply 'Bond Street'. When canvassed, of the seventy-seven occupants of Old Bond Street, only five were in favour. The result was less overwhelming at the other end of the street, but even so the parvenus voted 104 to 61 against being amalgamated with their fuddy-duddy neighbours.

Burlington Arcade

Richard Boyle (1612–98) was the Earl of Cork and Burlington, and the original Burlington House – an extended version of which now houses the Royal Academy on PICCADILLY – was his residence. Built at the same time as Clarendon House (see ALBEMARLE STREET), it backed on to open fields: Horace Walpole (1717–97) recorded the almost certainly apocryphal story that 'when asked why he built his house so far out of town, he replied, because he was determined to have no building beyond him'. There were still fields to the north in 1720, but by that time development was going on apace (see BOND STREET) and Richard's descendants soon found themselves in a built-up area. Various streets that were built in his backyard recall his family titles: Cork Street is one, and there is an Old Burlington Street, and a New Burlington Street, Place and Mews. Nor was his wife overlooked: Lady Burlington, née Lady Dorothy Savile, is remembered in Savile Row, home of elegant tailoring.

The covered shopping street known as Burlington Arcade is of later date (1819). By that time Burlington House was owned by Lord George Cavendish, whose brother, the Duke of Devonshire, had acquired it through marriage to a Burlington daughter. An 1817 edition of *The Gentleman's Magazine* gave several explanations for the proposed creation of the arcade: it was to be 'for the sale of jewellery and other fancy articles…for the gratification of the publick, and to give employment to industrious females'. But, the magazine went on to say, 'What first gave birth to the idea was the great annoyance to which the garden [of Burlington House] is subject from the inhabitants of a neighbouring street throwing oyster-shells etc. over the walls.' It seems unlikely that the residents of elegant BOND STREET should have made a habit of throwing their detritus over a neighbour's garden wall, but such seems to have been the case: one version of the story even claims that dead cats found their way into the grounds of Burlington House.

Curzon Street

At the end of the seventeenth century Sir Nathaniel Curzon MP acquired the land on which the May Fair was held (see the introduction to this section, page 104), so early tenants of his development must have been among those who whined about the fair. It's probable that among the things they objected to were the irregular weddings performed on this street at the Curzon or Mayfair Chapel. A certain Reverend Keith would conduct the ceremony for anyone prepared to pay him a guinea (£1.05 in modern parlance). The most flagrant of these weddings occurred when the Duke of Hamilton married the nineteen-year-old Miss Elizabeth Gunning in the dead of night on Valentine's Day 1752. The marriage had been so impromptu (they seem to have eloped on the spur of the moment from a party at

Bedford House in BLOOMSBURY) that 'a ring of the bed curtain' had to be used in place of the more conventional wedding band.

Keith, who had been excommunicated by his ecclesiastical superiors ten years before but clearly didn't give a damn, was so notorious that the 1754 Marriage Act was brought in largely to put a stop to him. Thereafter and for the first time, parental consent was required for the marriage of anyone under the age of twenty-one and, because the Act did not apply to Scotland, it led to young people in a hurry eloping to Gretna Green, just across the border.

Before we leave Elizabeth Gunning, it is worth recording that if titles were what she was after, she did pretty well. When her first husband died she married the son of the Duke of Argyll, who in due course inherited his father's title. Her eldest son became Duke of Hamilton when he was only three, but died young and was succeeded by his brother. Of the two sons of Elizabeth's second marriage who grew to adulthood, the elder died childless and was again succeeded by his brother. So in addition to marrying two dukes, she gave birth to four. Not bad for someone who had to borrow a dress from the local theatre company in order to have something decent to wear to her first grand party.

Running from Curzon Street down to PICCADILLY, the intriguingly named Half Moon Street, home of the fictional hero Bulldog Drummond, is called after a pub.

Dover Street

Henry Jermyn junior (c. 1636–1708), nephew of the one who created JERMYN STREET, was granted the title Baron Dover by James II. Dover Street, part of Sir Thomas Bond's development (see BOND STREET), was named after the substantial house he built here. When his widow died in 1726, Dover House was sold by auction and described in the

Daily Journal as 'consisting of seven rooms on a floor, with closets, a large and beautiful stair-case finely painted by Mr Laguerre, with 3 coach-houses and stables for 10 horses, and all manner of conveniences for a great family'. It's not there now, but the Arts Club a few doors up gives an idea of what it must have been like.

Grosvenor Square

The Grosvenor Estate, which covered the land on which Grosvenor Square now sits and a good bit more besides, belonged in the eighteenth century to one Sir Thomas Grosvenor of Eaton Hall in Cheshire, who had acquired it through marriage to a wealthy lady named Audley. Thus, when the square that bears his name was laid out in the 1720s under the auspices of Thomas's son Richard, it seemed only right to name two of the streets running out of it North and South Audley Street.

Thomas, Richard and their descendants were rich men – see BELGRAVIA for the further development of the Grosvenor Estate 100 years later.

The name Grosvenor comes from Norman French and means 'great hunter'. The French origin (linked to the modern word *gros*, 'fat') explains why the *s* in the middle of the name is not pronounced.

Hanover Square

Queen Anne died in 1714 with no surviving children (poor woman, she had had fourteen of them, but the only one to make it past infancy died at eleven). For complicated reasons involving the Stuart family tree, politically motivated marriages and the British establishment's paranoid fear of Catholics (see the Introduction, page 9), a German cousin was then invited to rule Great Britain. His title on his home territory being the

Elector of Hanover, he instituted the British House of Hanover and became known as George I. The three kings who followed him were also called George and everything that we now call Georgian – the style of architecture, furniture *et al.* – is down to them.

Hanover Square was laid out in the early years of the first George's reign and George Street runs into it. It was a happy coincidence that the new king should share his name with England's patron saint, so it was largely in compliment to the royal George that the church in the new development – where people who don't quite merit Westminster Abbey are married to this day – was dedicated to the saintly one.

The same royalism was taken rather further at St George's in BLOOMSBURY. The church is regarded by many as the architect Nicholas Hawksmoor's masterpiece, but some feel he overdid it by putting a statue of George I dressed as a Roman soldier and posing as his saintly namesake on the top of its obelisk. The writer Horace Walpole called it a 'master-stroke of absurdity' and a contemporary wit coined the epigram:

> *When Henry VIII left the Pope in the lurch,*
> *The Protestants made him the head of the church;*
> *But George's good subjects, the Bloomsbury people,*
> *Instead of the church made him head of the steeple.*

Hyde Park

'Hide' is one of the Domesday Book's favourite words: it means the amount of land needed to support a family. Initially, therefore, it wasn't a fixed measurement, because it varied according to such factors as the fertility of the land, but in due course it came to mean about 120 acres (49 hectares). So the subdivision of the manor of EBURY recorded in the thirteenth century as La Hyde would originally have been about that size. It must have extended over the years, though, because by the time Henry VIII took it over and turned it into a hunting ground in the 1530s, it covered its current area, almost 140 hectares. Since Charles II's time it has been a public park and was once the in place for the fashionable to walk, ride, drive their carriages and show off their new clothes. The Serpentine lake inside the park was created in the 1730s by diverting and damming a local brook and joining up several existing ponds. The resulting body of water takes its name from its (vaguely) snake-like shape. See also ROTTEN ROW.

Hyde Park Corner – the south-eastern corner of the park, where PARK LANE meets KNIGHTSBRIDGE – once boasted a tollgate, where a main road from the west entered WESTMINSTER. This made it a sufficiently important landmark for the name to be recorded as early as the 1550s.

Marble Arch

Well, it's an arch and it's made of marble. What more do you want to know?

Oh, all right then.

First of all, Marble Arch wasn't always where it is now. Inspired by the Arch of Constantine in Rome, it was designed – by John Nash (1752–1835), he of REGENT STREET fame – as part of the grand approach to BUCKINGHAM PALACE, which George IV was doing up to suit his extravagant tastes. The plan was that you would be able to sweep out of HYDE PARK, through the arch to be built for the purpose, drive down the side of GREEN PARK and through this second arch into the grounds of the palace itself. It never quite worked out that way, the arch got in the way of further extensions to the palace and it was moved to its current site in 1851.

The idea of having a fancy arch at the western end of OXFORD STREET shows just how far up in the world the area had come: from medieval times to 1783, this place – known as Tyburn for reasons explained under MARYLEBONE – was the site of public hangings, often accompanied by drawing, quartering and disembowelling. In the sixteenth century the infamous 'Tyburn tree' was erected here: it was a triangular frame capable of hanging twenty-four people at a time. Public hangings were supposed to act as a deterrent to the criminally minded; in fact they became the excuse for rowdy and drunken fairs. Crowds lined the route from Newgate Prison in the City to cheer and jeer the executees. In 1725, these included Jonathan Wild, highwayman turned 'thief taker', who was rumoured to shop his own men for a two-pound reward. By the time Wild was brought to justice he was so notorious that tickets, illustrated with an engraving of the condemned man, were sold in advance for the best vantage points at his hanging.

Fun though this obviously was for the masses, all good things must come to an end. As London expanded westward and the prosperous West End came into being, influential locals campaigned successfully to have the riff-raff removed from their neighbourhood; executions were moved to the more confined quarters of Newgate Prison, where the authorities had a better chance of keeping the crowds under control. Perhaps they should try moving some of today's Saturday shoppers over there too.

Park Lane

So named because it runs along the eastern side of HYDE PARK. A lane that had linked Hyde Park Corner to Tyburn (see MARBLE ARCH) for centuries was upgraded in the eighteenth century; it was in the early nineteenth that most of the existing grand buildings were built or extended, earning the street its reputation for desirable real estate.

Regent Street/Regent's Park

If you have seen *The Madness of King George*, you'll remember that George III (1760–1820) went mad. (If you haven't, the title of the film may give you a clue.) His eldest son, also George, was officially made Regent in 1811 and ruled in his father's place for the last years of the latter's life. The Regent, later George IV (1820–30), was by all accounts a thoroughly nasty piece of work – extravagant, self-indulgent and a disloyal friend – but there is no denying that he was a great patron of art and architecture. Anybody who has visited the Royal Pavilion in Brighton may have doubts about his taste (if you wanted to leave a memorial dedicated to your extravagance and self-indulgence, this is what you would build), but this aberration notwithstanding there is one thing that will stand to his eternal credit. He took the architect John Nash (1752–1835) under his wing.

It was Nash who laid out Regent Street, as a link from the Regent's residence at Carlton House, on the fringes of St James's Park, to what became known as the Regent's Park. (In fact, Regent Street stops halfway between Oxford Street and the park: it becomes Portland Place, which already existed and which Nash incorporated into his plans.) All Soul's Church, at the junction of Portland Place and Regent Street, is the only surviving Nash building in the immediate environs, though anyone wanting to admire more of the architect's genius has only to walk a few hundred metres north and look at the various terraces on the fringes of the park. The street, the park and the Regency style of architecture that Nash perfected are all named after his royal patron. He was also responsible for much of the architecture of the Brighton Pavilion, but can't be blamed for the excesses of the interior.

Rotten Row

Established in HYDE PARK during the reign of William III (1689–1702), Rotten Row was intended to provide easy and safe access between ST JAMES'S Palace and KENSINGTON Palace, where William chose to spend most of his time. It was wide enough for three carriages to pass each other in comfort, which makes it tempting to steal a few lines from the musical *Fiddler on the Roof* and suggest that there was one going east, one going west and one more going nowhere just for show. Certainly by the early nineteenth century Rotten Row was the place for the fashionable, with their new clothes and carriages, to see and be seen.

As for the name of the 'row' or avenue, the commonly held view that it derived from the French *route du roi*, 'road of the king', seems unlikely to be true. After all, William III was Dutch and spent much of his reign at war with France: French was not the fashionable language of the time. More probable is that 'rotten' was simply a colloquial description of the row's sandy, gravelly soil – the OED gives this definition, current at the period: 'of ground, soil, etc.: lacking structure or cohesion; excessively soft, loose, or boggy'. Not very glamorous, perhaps, but what can you do?

Shepherd Market

Whatever else they may sell in Shepherd Market (it has had its share of dealers in one of the older professions), it has never been sheep: it is named after Edward Shepherd (died 1747), the architect and developer who was commissioned to smarten up this part of MAYFAIR once the scandalous fair had moved on. His two-storey market, now mostly occupied by restaurants and art galleries, is still the focal point of the square that bears his name.

SOHO

One way of reminding ourselves how unbuilt-up much of the City of WESTMINSTER used to be is to consider the number of places that have – or had until surprisingly recently – the word 'field' in their name (see, for example, ST GILES and LEICESTER SQUARE). Another is to realise that 'Soho' is a hunting cry, originally announcing the sighting of a hare. It comes from Anglo-French, like many things associated with upper-class recreation after the Norman Conquest.

Soho Fields, a hunting ground in the sixteenth century, were also an important source of water: in 1671 a proclamation was issued prohibiting the building of any more 'small habitations and cottages' in the fields adjoining 'So-Hoe', because the buildings 'choak up the air of his Majesty's palaces and parks, and endanger the total loss of the waters, which, by expensive conduits, etc., are conveyed from those fields to his Majesty's Palace at WHITEHALL'. Clearly nobody took a blind bit of notice, because a mere four years later the area was so built up that it had to have its own 'rates receiver' to collect local taxes. Perhaps the builders got round the regs by putting up not 'small habitations' but mansions – there was certainly no shortage of those. Soho Square was originally called King Square, after Charles II, but had taken its modern name by 1720, when Strype tells us that it cost a shilling (5p) to take a hackney coach here from Westminster Hall.

Berwick Street

Probably named after the Duke of Berwick (1670–1734), an illegitimate son of James II and a patron of the local developer, a fellow Catholic named James Pollett. Assuming this is correct, it is surprising that the name should have survived. Being a Catholic became more or less illegal after James II was deposed at the end of 1688; Berwick followed his father into exile, ended up fighting for the French against the English, was subsequently attainted and forfeited all his British titles; yet a street named after him has hung in there. Odd. But no one seems to have come up with a better explanation.

Carnaby Street

According to Strype, the east side of Carnaby Street boasted an unusual feature: 'the Earl of Craven's Pest-houses, seated in a large piece of ground, enclosed with a brick wall, and handsomely set with trees, in which are buildings for the entertainment of persons that shall have the plague, when it shall please God that any contagion shall happen'. 'Pest' here is a synonym for 'plague' and 'entertainment' means 'maintenance'; the Earl's philanthropy, considerable though it was, didn't extend to putting on theatrical performances for the benefit of the inmates.

I tell you this because it is more clear-cut than the origin of Carnaby. The imposing Karnaby House was built hereabouts in 1683, presumably for someone called Karnaby, but who he was remains a mystery. The street, which seems always to have used the modern spelling, was laid out only a year or two later. Karnaby House must have gone by 1720, when Strype was writing, because the Pest-houses were either on the same site or far too close to it to make desirable neighbours.

Coventry Street

Named after Coventry House, the residence of Henry Coventry (1619–86), Secretary of State to Charles II.

Dean Street

The origins of this name are surprisingly vague. They are almost certainly ecclesiastical, but no one seems to be sure which Dean was being honoured. Henry Compton (1632–1713), Bishop of London and Dean of the Chapels Royal, is the most likely candidate. Certainly the timing is right, as he held both these offices in the 1670s and '80s, when SOHO was being developed. If this is true, the area suffers from a not uncommon dose of overkill, as Old Compton Street and New Compton Street are named after the same bishop.

Foubert's Place

This little alley running into CARNABY STREET is named after a Major Foubert, a Frenchman who, according to Evelyn in 1681, was 'lately come from Paris for his religion, and resolving to settle here'. He must have been a Protestant – a bad thing to be in France at that time.

Foubert set up a military riding academy, sponsored by Charles II and attracting all the young gallants of the day. He taught not only riding but such necessary additions to a gentleman's education as flinging a javelin, firing a pistol at a target and picking up a gauntlet on the point of a sword, all while riding at full speed. The academy was highly successful: the Duke of Cumberland, who went on to massacre the Scots at Culloden, was a pupil there in 1731 and nearly a century later the name survived when much of the surrounding area was demolished to make way for REGENT STREET.

Frith Street

Richard Frith was a building speculator, responsible for much of the development in this part of SOHO in the 1680s. As the most casual glance over the ST JAMES'S section of this book will show you, he was not the only developer to name a street after himself.

Glasshouse Street

Glass houses or factories abounded in London in the seventeenth century; it may not be a coincidence that this one was conveniently close to Brewer Street. Just round the corner was a street known as Knaves Acre (not hard to speculate as to why), which Strype tells us 'is but narrow, and chiefly inhabited by those that deal in old Goods, and Glass Bottles'. It doesn't sound as if it rivalled Murano, somehow.

Golden Square

The antiquary Thomas Pennant (1726–98) wrote an *Account of London* in which he reported that this square was 'originally called Gelding Square, from the sign of a neighbouring inn; but the inhabitants, indignant at the vulgarity of the name, changed it to the present'. There seems to have been a 'Gelding Field' nearby in the 1570s, presumably a place where horses were kept; the royal licence to build on the area, signed by Christopher Wren in 1673, refers to 'Gelding Close'. The name 'Golden Square' appears as early as 1688 and 'Golding Square' in 1690. The last of these is said to be 'so called from the first builder' but is more likely to be a clerical error. The idea that the new residents were trying to move themselves up market is surely the most plausible one.

Greek Street

There was a Greek community here in the seventeenth century and the street takes its name from the local church, the first Greek Orthodox one in London. The huge influx of French Protestants to London in general and SOHO in particular shortly afterwards led to the church's being taken over by them; it was demolished in 1936. At that time, the inscription that had been built into the wall was salvaged and can now be seen in the Greek Orthodox Cathedral of Saint Sophia in BAYS-WATER, whose address, incongruously, is Moscow Road.

Leicester Square

The title Earl of Leicester has been created a number of times throughout English history, because the male line keeps dying out. Most famously, Queen Elizabeth created it for her favourite, Robert Dudley, in 1564, but that is not the family that concerns us here. The first seventeenth-century Earl of Leicester was Robert Sidney, a nephew of Robert Dudley and brother of Philip Sidney, the Elizabethan poet and soldier. It was this earl's son, also Robert (1595–1677), who built himself a mansion on land that he bought from the parish of St Martin's. Part of this land had always been open to the poor of the parish at Lammas-tide (around 1 August), and it was integral to the deal that Robert should continue to accommodate them. The land that remained open became known as Leicester Field and, when it was later built up, as Leicester Square. Strype, writing in 1720, tells us that it is 'a very handsome, large square, enclosed with rails, and graced on all sides with good built houses, well inhabited, and resorted unto by gentry'. By 'well inhabited' he clearly means 'by a desirable class of person', as he goes on to mention the residences of not one but two earls. The peerage, of course, has long since moved out to make way for a barrage of cinemas.

Oxford Street

Once upon a time, Tyburn (see MARBLE ARCH) was about as far west as most Londoners ever went, so it was logical to call the road leading to it Tyburn Road. Times changed and the city expanded so that people now lived near Tyburn rather than merely traipsing out to witness an execution. By the same token, travelling to a city 100 kilometres away was no longer beyond most people's wildest imaginings. More importantly, the name Tyburn was inextricably associated with the gallows, while Oxford had a posher ring to it, and thus Oxford Road was born. The coincidental fact that the Earl of Oxford owned land nearby also influenced the change. Daniel Defoe, writing in 1725, records that:

> ...*a new bear garden...being a stage for the Gladiators or prize-fighters, is built on the Tyburn Road. N.B. The gentlemen of the science [that is, upper-crust boxing fans] taking offence at its being called Tyburn Road, though it really is so, will have it called the Oxford Road.*

The gentlemen boxing fans soon had their way: the writer Thomas Pennant, reminiscing about his youth in about the 1740s, calls the street 'Oxford Street' without reference to Tyburn, but remembers it is as 'a deep hollow road, and full of sloughs; with here and there a ragged house, the lurking place of cut-throats'. Not much change there, then.

New Oxford Street, a continuation of the east end of Oxford Street, was opened in 1847, having been built over part of the 'rookery' of ST GILES. A contemporary commentator tells us, with remarkable precision, that it cost £290,227.4s.10d., over £100,000 of which went into the pocket of the Duke of Bedford (see RUSSELL SQUARE), who owned much of the freehold.

Poland Street

Perhaps surprisingly, giving how cosmopolitan Soho was in the seventeenth century (see GREEK STREET), this street doesn't seem to take its name from a Polish community. It is more likely that it was called after a pub, the King of Poland, whose name celebrated the victory of the Holy League over the Turks at Vienna in 1683.

If that seems like a tenuous link, it may help you to know that the army of the Holy League was on that occasion commanded by the King of Poland, Jan III Sobieski, and that the Holy League was a multinational Christian army formed specifically to resist the spread of the Ottoman (Turkish) Empire. Given that in those days the Turks were generally perceived as the bad guys of Europe, naming a pub in celebration of a victory over them was reasonable enough.

Romilly Street

A little street that earns a mention because of this story about Sir Samuel Romilly (1757–1818), after whom it is named. According to one nineteenth-century commentator, 'Romilly entered the House of Commons in 1806, the electors of Westminster having returned him to Parliament without the expenditure of a shilling on his part; a great thing in those days of bribery and corruption.' He became an important legal reformer and was almost single-handedly responsible for reducing the vast number of crimes on the English statute book (225 in 1815) for which the punishment was death. It is largely thanks to Sam that you can no longer be hanged for shoplifting, stealing from a rabbit warren or being out at night with a blackened face.

Rupert Street

Prince Rupert of the Rhine (1619–82) was a nephew of Charles I and the leader of the Royalist cavalry during the Civil War. Exiled after Charles's defeat, he returned to England after the Restoration in 1660 and became a naval commander during Charles II's wars against the Dutch. So he was a national hero just at the time when Rupert Street was looking for a name.

Wardour Street

Henry Arundell, third Baron Arundell of Wardour (c. 1607–94) was a devout Catholic at a time when this was a risky thing to be, and as such was a loyal supporter of James II. When the king was deposed in 1688 and the Protestants William and Mary took the throne, Henry prudently retired to his country seat and took no further part in public life. But at the peak of his career he had been a member of James's Privy Council and a considerable landowner in the part of SOHO that was being developed at the time. So, as with the Duke of BERWICK, his memory lingers on.

Windmill Street

There are several Windmill Streets in London, but the one just off PICCADILLY Circus is officially Great Windmill Street. It is named after the windmill that stood here until the eighteenth century and led to this area being known (before anyone thought of building anything more comfortable than a windmill on it) as Windmill Fields. One of the developers was a Colonel Panton, who was, according to a nineteenth-century report, 'one of those rare personages, successful gamesters'. His name is remembered in a street off LEICESTER SQUARE.

The Windmill Theatre, famous for its nude tableaux and for resolutely refusing to close during the Second World War, remained in business until 1964 and the building now houses a table-dancing nightclub. It doesn't look like a windmill, though – for that you need to go to WIMBLEDON Common, where an 1817 windmill now houses the Windmill Museum.

WESTMINSTER NORTH

This is perhaps the surprising part - the bit you might not have realised was in Westminster. With Regent's Park (covered under REGENT STREET in the previous chapter) as its easternmost point, north Westminster extends all the way west to such distant-sounding postal districts as NW8 and W9. It nevertheless contains its share of familiar names.

Abbey Road

Yes, there was an abbey here, long before there was a Beatles album. About 839 years before, in fact – KILBURN Priory was established around 1130 AD. A priory is normally an offshoot of an abbey, and Kilburn Priory was founded under the auspices of WESTMINSTER Abbey. So, appropriately enough, there is still also a Priory Road just off Abbey Road.

Baker Street

A nineteenth-century chronicler's list of Baker Street's famous residents includes the actress Mrs Siddons (see GARRICK STREET); the all-but-forgotten poet Alexander Boswell, son of Johnson's biographer; William Pitt the Elder; and Madame Tussaud. Little did he know that within a generation these would all be overshadowed by a certain fictional consulting detective, whose museum is today labelled Number 221B, although it sits between Numbers 237 and 241. A surprising number of people still write to Sherlock Holmes at this address, ignoring the facts that a) he never existed in the first place and b) even if he had, and you accept that he survived the Reichenbach Falls and lived to a ripe old age, he would have been dead for about seventy years. It shows the power of fiction – and, of course, latterly of television: Sherlock is, at a conservative estimate, twenty million times more famous than Sir Edward Baker, the eighteenth-century builder responsible for laying out and giving a name to the street.

Bayswater

The name 'Bayard's watering place' is recorded as early as 1380, when this area was a goodish way out of town and horses that had started their journey in the City might have been glad to stop for a drink. *Bayard* was originally a word for a bay-coloured horse but, as it seems unlikely that there were separate watering holes for greys and chestnuts, Bayard was probably the name of the local landowner or the man in charge of the watering place.

A digression: the Oxford English Dictionary records a seventeenth-century idiom *bayard of ten toes*, first used about 150 years before *Shanks's pony* but meaning the same thing – one's own feet, the only means of conveyance a poor man could afford.

Edgware Road

Although it changes name a couple of times along the way, Edgware Road basically runs from MARBLE ARCH to Edgware, on the fringes of North London. It covers part of the ancient Roman road known as Watling Street, which continued all the way to Wroxeter in Shropshire, much of it along the route of today's A5. The name is an Old English one, dating back to the tenth century. The ending comes from the same source as the modern word 'weir' and Edgware was a weir or fishing enclosure associated with a man called Ecgi. Sadly, as with many Old English place names connected with a person, we know nothing whatever about Mr Ecgi. Except, presumably, that he fished.

Harley Street

Edward Harley, second Earl of Oxford (1689–1741), was a friend and neighbour of Sir Richard Grosvenor (see GROSVENOR SQUARE) and began to develop land that he owned north of OXFORD STREET at about the time that Richard was doing the same thing to the south. The street that is now synonymous with the private medical profession bears his name, but his influence can be seen in many other streets round about. In addition to being Earl of Oxford, Edward also held the titles Earl Mortimer and Baron Wigmore, owned an estate in Cambridgeshire called Wimpole and another in Northamptonshire called Welbeck. His wife was Lady Henrietta Cavendish Holles and their daughter Margaret married the Duke of Portland (see PORTLAND PLACE). Wander the streets behind John Lewis and you will see that all these names crop up. The Wigmore Hall concert venue is so named because it is in Wigmore Street.

Lancaster Gate

The Duchy of Lancaster is one of two royal duchies; the other is Cornwall, whose duke is the Prince of Wales. The reigning monarch, of whichever gender, holds the title Duke of Lancaster (there hasn't been a separate Duke of Lancaster since the Wars of the Roses; if you know anything about that little local difficulty, you'll probably agree that it is just as well). It follows, therefore, that Queen Victoria held the title Duke of Lancaster. When, in the 1850s, a new gate was needed on the north side of KENSINGTON Gardens, there was already a Victoria Gate just up the road. But as it seems to have crossed nobody's mind that any new structure could be named other than after the queen and her consort, one of her subsidiary titles was adopted instead.

The elegant street just across BAYSWATER Road was built only a few years later and takes its name from the gate.

Little Venice

The poet Robert Browning (1812–89) moved back to England from Italy after his wife Elizabeth Barrett Browning died in 1861. He settled in this pretty part of MAIDA VALE, where the Regent's Canal joins the Grand Union. He is widely credited with having coined the nickname, though there seems to be no record of the original context. But then a remark likening a place that happens to have canals to Venice is not necessarily going to make it into a book of collected wit and wisdom. Robert certainly lived here for most of the last twenty-five years of his life and is commemorated in the nearby Browning's Pool.

Maida Vale

Just as pubs called the Nelson sprang up all over the country after the admiral's death at the Battle of Trafalgar in 1805 (see TRAFALGAR SQUARE), so the following year there was a fashion for calling them the Hero of Maida. Maida, in southern Italy, was the site of a British victory against the allies of Napoleon, which did much to restore morale after the crushing defeat of Austerlitz a few months earlier (the French are proud of that one – there is a station in Paris named after it, so they obviously feel the same way about it as we do about

Waterloo). Anyway, the Hero of Maida was the now largely forgotten General Sir John Stuart. The pub in Maida Vale commemorating him has long since vanished, but it lasted long enough to give its name to the street on which it stood (an extension of EDGWARE ROAD). In the 1820s this was known as Maida Hill; by the 1860s it was Maida Vale – *vale* being a poetic word for *valley* and presumably referring to the bit at the bottom of Maida Hill – and the name has since extended to the area around it.

Manchester Square

In 1776 the fourth Duke of Manchester (1737–88) had a fine house built for himself on this site; it was later taken over by the Marquesses of Hertford, a family with a marked talent for acquiring works of art, furniture and armour. Their fabulous horde has become the Wallace Collection, named after Richard Wallace, illegitimate son and heir of the fourth Marquess: it was Richard's widow who, in 1897, presented the collection to the nation.

Despite its elegance, Manchester Square was one of a number in the area built over a sewer that as late as the nineteenth century was emitting 'the most disgusting effluvium' and thus rendering its inhabitants vulnerable to typhus and attack by rats. It wasn't only the poor who benefited from the major clean-up job that London underwent in Victorian times.

Marylebone

The river Tyburn, now largely underground, runs roughly north–south from HAMPSTEAD to enter the Thames at PIMLICO. In medieval times it marked the boundary between two manors – hence its name, which means 'boundary stream'. In the fifteenth century a church dedicated to the Virgin Mary was built here and the area became known as Maryburne – 'Mary by the stream'. The original St Mary's has been demolished and its site is now a garden of rest at the north end of Marylebone High Street; the much larger parish church on Marylebone Road is a nineteenth-century replacement, built to accommodate a vastly increased population.

Since the fifteenth century, two notable changes in Marylebone's name have come about: the le has been introduced, possibly by analogy with St-Mary-le-Bow (see BOW LANE) and meaning loosely 'the one at or near…'; and the r of burn has disappeared, almost certainly for simplicity's sake: having an r in the first part of the word and again in the second would have made it something of a tongue twister. One of the cardinal rules of place-name development is that if a name is difficult to pronounce, it will, over the years, evolve into something easier – as this one duly did, to produce what most of us now call 'Marlibone'.

Montagu Square

This is worth a mention because Elizabeth Montagu (1718–1800), who built Montagu House, after which the square is named, was one of the original 'bluestockings'. With her friend Elizabeth Vesey she held literary salons which became famous for shunning alcohol and cards, and making conversation the focal point of the entertainment. Most of the members were women, but Dr Johnson, the painter Sir Joshua Reynolds and the writer Horace Walpole were among many men who attended by invitation. The bluestockings were really early feminists: they were interested in improving educational opportunities for women and giving them more choice in the way they lived their lives.

The origin of the name 'bluestocking' is much disputed, but the favoured (though probably untrue) story derives from the fact that men

wore blue stockings, made of worsted, only during the day; a fashionable gentleman would change these for black silk in the evening. The
botanist Benjamin Stillingfleet, invited to attend one of the ladies'
salons, pointed out that he was not a wealthy man and did not own
the correct attire for an evening party. 'Oh, come in your blue stockings,' the two Elizabeths may or may not have said. Interesting, then,
that 'bluestocking' is now a term applied to an intellectual woman,
when it was poor old Ben who first broke the sartorial rules.

Paddington

Padda, like the Ecgi who gave his name to EDGWARE ROAD, was an
Anglo-Saxon about whom we know nothing. But he or his family or
followers had a farmstead or estate in this part of town in the tenth
century or so, and that is what the name means. The station,
designed by Isambard Kingdom Brunel, opened in 1854. The great
engineer's statue now shares pride of place with that of a fictional
teddy bear, a refugee from Darkest Peru, who took his name from
the station on which he was found because no one would understand
his Peruvian one.

MAINLINE STATIONS

Cannon Street is connected not with cannons, nor even with
canons, but with candlemakers: this street and the ward in
which it sits was once called Candlewick or Candlewright and
was mentioned as the former in a Coroner's Roll from the reign
of Edward I (1272–1307). Its corruption into its modern form
(which had happened by Pepys' time) is a prime example of one

of the basic rules of place-name evolution: if a name can be garbled and made shorter, it will be. The station opened in 1866.

Euston is Old English, meaning 'farmstead of a man called Efe', but it turned up in London in Georgian times because it is the name of the country estate, near Thetford, in Suffolk, of the Dukes of Grafton (see FITZROY SQUARE). Euston (originally Euston Square) mainline station was opened in 1837.

Fenchurch Street is recorded (as Fanchurche) in 1276 and the name refers either to a church on fenny or marshy ground or to one near the hay market (*faenum* in Latin). It is not certain that there was ever a fen here, but there may be some long-lost connection with the moor outside the City walls (see MOORGATE). There is known to have been a church here in the early fourteenth century – St Gabriel Fenchurch, which was destroyed in the Great Fire of 1666 and not rebuilt. Given that new churches were very frequently built on the site of old ones, there could easily have been a church there in time to give the area its name. The railway station was opened in 1841. And, for those who care about this sort of trivia, Fenchurch Street is the only London terminus that does not have its own Underground station – in order to get on the tube you have to walk round the corner to Tower Hill.

Liverpool Street was, from 1246, the site of a priory dedicated to St Mary of Bethlehem which later became, according to Stow, 'an Hospitall for distracted people'. This asylum, known as the Bethlehem Royal Hospital (or Bedlam, hence the modern word), moved a number of times: for much of the nineteenth and early twentieth centuries it was south of the river, in LAMBETH, where the surviving part of its building now houses the Imperial War Museum. But its original site and the winding lane of houses that was built there continued to be known as Old Bethlehem. When this street was widened and the houses substantially rebuilt in 1829, it was renamed Liverpool Street, in honour of the recently deceased Prime Minister Lord Liverpool. The railway station came into being in 1874.

London Bridge was for many centuries the only bridge across the Thames below KINGSTON and therefore a vital link between the City and all points south. It was also a thriving community in its own right, with houses and shops lining both sides from the thirteenth century until the 1750s, when they were decreed to be both a fire hazard and a major cause of congestion and were demolished. The medieval bridge was replaced in the 1830s by something wider, though Wheatley, writing in the 1890s, remarks that the new bridge 'has proved insufficient for the ever-increasing traffic'. No change there, then. The railway station London Bridge opened in 1836, making it the oldest of the London termini.

St Pancras is reckoned to be one of the oldest places of Christian worship in England and was the established name of the local parish when the station was opened in 1868. The oldest church on the site just round the corner pre-dates the arrival of St Augustine in Canterbury in the year 597, so may have been founded by the early missionaries mentioned under BRIDEWELL PLACE/ST BRIDE'S. It may be Augustine who brought the name with him, though: in Rome he had lived near the Basilica of St Pancratius, to give him his Latin name, and the suggestion is that he (Augustine) was eager to spread his (St Pancratius') cult. Pancratius had converted to Christianity in defiance of the wishes of the Emperor Diocletian and was beheaded in 304, when he was about fourteen years old.

Victoria – named after the queen, obviously. But as with Waterloo (see below), the street came first, cutting through the slums of WESTMINSTER in the 1850s. The station was opened in 1860. Our longest-reigning monarch has any number of streets, roads and avenues named after her, not to mention the thoroughfare that most Londoners call merely The Embankment (see VICTORIA EMBANKMENT), a substantial park in the East End and a goodly handful of pubs all over the capital. Basically, if it has Victoria in its name, chances are it means her.

Waterloo is named after the battle, in 1815, in which Napoleon was finally defeated and the Duke of Wellington became a national hero. The first thing to be named 'Waterloo' was a new bridge across the Thames, opened in 1817; then came the road at its southern approach; the station followed in 1848 and finally the whole area took on the name. Waterloo was and is, of course, the place in Belgium where the battle was fought: its name may mean 'watery clearing'.

For King's Cross, see the box *Which King, Which Queen?* on page 155; and see individual entries for BLACKFRIARS, CHARING CROSS, MARYLEBONE and PADDINGTON.

Portland Place

Not to be confused with PORTMAN SQUARE, this and Great and Little Portland Streets are named after the local landlord, the Duke of Portland (1738–1809), who served two brief terms as Prime Minister, in 1783 and in 1807–9. Portland Place, designed by the Adam brothers in the 1770s, served as an inspiration to Nash when he laid out REGENT STREET fifty years later. At the time of the development, a former MP called Lord Foley had a mansion at the southern end of Portland Place and the story goes that the street is as wide as it is (very wide for a city street, in case you don't know it) because the Duke honoured a promise to Lord Foley not to impede the view from his house.

Before succeeding to the dukedom, Lord Portland had been known as the Marquess of Titchfield, a courtesy title that passed to his own eldest son and explains the presence of Great and Little Titchfield Streets in the immediate vicinity. There's also a Foley Street not far away. And see HARLEY STREET for some more of Lord Portland's friends and relations.

Portman Square

Another area developed on the estate of once-rich families who needed the money. Henry Portman starting leasing off property in the 1750s, was wise enough to choose Robert Adam, one of the famous Adam brothers, as one of his architects and produced some very beautiful and expensive houses.

St John's Wood

If you don't know who the Knights Hospitaller were, please flip forward a few pages and look at the box *In the Name of the Law* on page 139.

Okay? Are you with me?

Well, that order was also known as the Knights of St John, and they owned this heavily wooded area in the fourteenth century. It was a royal hunting ground from the time of Henry VIII (1509–47) until at least James I (1603–25): there is a record dated 1616 of one Robert Stacy being paid £20 a year 'for keeping the King's deer in St John's Wood, co. Middlesex'. The trees were later cut down by order of that renowned killjoy, Oliver Cromwell.

CAMDEN

Camden Town was one of the many areas of 'ribbon development' that grew up along the main roads out of London in the late eighteenth and early nineteenth centuries. The name comes indirectly from the great antiquarian William Camden (1551–1623), who in the 1580s wrote the first topography of Britain. In later life Camden settled near CHISLEHURST and in the eighteenth century his former estate – known as Camden Place – came into the possession of Charles Pratt (1714–94), a successful lawyer and politician who was given the titles Baron and later Earl of Camden. A wealthy man, he owned a substantial area of land just north of London which in 1791 he divided into plots and leased for the development of what is now Camden Town. Nor does his legacy end there: turn east off the High Street just north of MORNINGTON CRESCENT and you will find yourself in Pratt Street.

Much of the modern borough lies within what most people would think of as central London, and it is that area that concerns us first.

HOLBORN

The Fleet River, mentioned under FLEET STREET, rises – as many London rivers do – in HAMPSTEAD and wends its way down through

NWI, WCI and ECI to reach the Fleet Street area. En route, it under-
goes a few changes of name, and at the point where it crosses
Holborn it is called the Holborn. The *-born* ending is, despite the
spelling, the same as the *-bourn* or *-bourne* of the Westbourne (see
WESTBOURNE GROVE/WESTBOURNE PARK) and means 'stream'. *Hol* comes
from the same root as the modern word *hollow*, so Holborn was
'the stream in the hollow'. There was once a street named Holborn
Hill: it ceased to exist after Holborn Viaduct was built in the 1860s,
but the Holborn ran through the hollow at the bottom of the hill.

Hatton Garden

Sir Christopher Hatton (1540–91) was Lord Chancellor in the reign
of Elizabeth I and was buried in the old St Paul's Cathedral, where
Stow tells us he had 'a most sumptuous monument' close to the tombs
of Sir Philip Sidney and Sir Francis Walsingham, both also prominent
Elizabethan courtiers. On this monument 'a merry poet' had written:

> *Philip and Francis haue no Tombe,*
> *For great Christopher takes all the roome.*

A favourite of the queen's, Christopher had been a wealthy man and
had a grand mansion, Hatton House, just north of what is now
HOLBORN. It had gone by the early eighteenth century and the name
Hatton Garden was being applied to a number of streets that had been
built on Christopher's former estate. Eventually narrowed down to a
single street, Hatton Garden remained 'an esteemed situation for the
gentry' until about 1800; a certain Miss Hawkins, writing her memoirs
in 1824, recalls a time when 'no shops were permitted but at the lower
end, and few parts of town could vie with it'. She goes on to lament
the fact that 'this situation, like all others in succession, is ruined by

trades and low associations'. Shame – if only she could have hung around another fifty years she would have heard about the discovery of diamonds in Kimberley in South Africa and seen the class of trades-man in Hatton Garden go up several notches as a result.

Anyone strolling down Hatton Garden today may be tempted to turn eastward into Greville Street and thence to Bleeding Heart Yard. The name of Greville Street merely recalls another Elizabethan courtier, but there is a suitably gory story attached to Bleeding Heart Yard. It concerns Lady Elizabeth Hatton, who had married Christo-pher's nephew and heir; on his death she married again but refused to take her husband's name and gained a reputation for being shall we say headstrong? Anyway, one night in January 1626, she is said to have gone to a ball at Hatton House and slipped away with a man who may or may not have been the Spanish ambassador. Her body was found the next morning in the cobbled yard behind the house. It was torn limb from limb, but her heart was still throbbing and pumping blood on to the cobbles. There is bound to be some symbolism there – a lesson to all married women who are tempted to run off with hand-some strangers on cold winter's nights – but for the life of me I can't work it out. Perhaps 'Just don't do it' sums it up.

Hatton Cross, that mysterious tube station on the way to Heathrow (does anyone *ever* get on or off there?), has a different derivation. It is 'the crossroads by the farmstead on the heath' – the same heath that contributed to the name of Heathrow.

IN THE NAME OF THE LAW

At the time of the Crusades – around 900 years ago – two military orders of Christian knights, who somehow reconciled it with their consciences to be both monks and warriors, became immensely influential across Europe. One was the Knights Hospitaller, so called because of their self-imposed mission to tend the sick. The other was the Knights Templar, who took their name from the Temple of Solomon in Jerusalem.

Establishing themselves in London, they built a monastic complex, including church, accommodation and military training ground, on land granted to them by the king, between FLEET STREET and the river. The Order of the Templars was suppressed in the early fourteenth century (they had become too darned wealthy for their own good) but their church, known to this day as the Temple Church, is still there and serves the communities of the **Inner** and **Middle Temple**, two of the four medieval Inns of Court.

The Inns of Court and their contemporaries the Inns of Chancery are called inns for a sensible historic reason – they provided accommodation as well as training for law students. They came into being from the thirteenth century, after two crises in the English legal profession. One, Henry III (1216–72) had forbidden the teaching of law within the City of London, so it had to be done elsewhere. The village – as it then was – of HOLBORN was conveniently situated for the law courts at WESTMINSTER. And two, the Pope had forbidden the clergy to teach common (secular) law rather than canon (church) law, so the whole issue of learning law was in turmoil.

There are believed once to have been ten Inns of Chancery, each attached to an Inn of Court 'like Maids of Honour to a Princess', as the fifteenth-century lawyer John Fortescue put it. Latterly they focused on the training of solicitors, whereas the Inns of Court were devoted to barristers. The Inns of Chancery have not survived as legal institutions, but some of the buildings that housed them live on and give their names to the lanes in which they stand:

- **Barnard's Inn** is something of a mystery: a seventeenth-century commentator tells us that 'being in the occupation of one Barnard, at the time of the conversion thereof into an Inne of Chauncery, it beareth Barnard's name still to this day'. But who Barnard was, no one seems to know.
- **Clement's Inn**, situated near ST CLEMENT DANES, took its name from the church and surrounding parish.
- **Clifford's Inn** was built on land granted to Robert Clifford by Edward II (1307–27) and let by his widow Isabel to what Stow called 'Students of the law'. It subsequently passed back and forth between the king and the Cliffords, but in Stow's time was let to the students for four pounds a year.
- **Staple Inn**, so called either because it was originally the Inn of the Merchants of the Staple (involved in the export of wool) or because it was built with pillars ('a post, pillar or stone' being a Middle English meaning of 'staple'). Stow says frankly, 'whereof so named I am ignorant'.

More famous are the other surviving Inns of Court, **Gray's Inn** and **Lincoln's Inn**. The former is named after the de Grey family who became the Barons Grey de Wilton and owned the local manor in the fourteenth century. The inn is known to date back to at least 1370. **Gray's Inn Road** is an ancient thoroughfare. It is recorded under an earlier name in 1234 and in its modern form in the early fifteenth century. Lincoln's Inn takes its name from the Earl of Lincoln, who encouraged lawyers to settle in this area after Henry III's decree mentioned above. Despite protests from the resident lawyers, **Lincoln's Inn Fields** were laid out as one of London's first licensed housing developments in the 1650s.

And, in case you are wondering why there isn't an Outer Temple, well, there was once. It is believed to have been one of the Inns of Chancery, but didn't last long – it was certainly not in existence in the seventeenth century. Unlike the other inns, it didn't have a great hall and that seems to have been the kiss of death.

Red Lion Square

The modern square takes its name from a much older pub with somewhat gruesome connections. In 1661 Oliver Cromwell and two others involved in the execution of Charles I spent the night at what is now the Old Red Lion Inn before being dragged through the streets and ritually hanged at Tyburn (see MARBLE ARCH). This wouldn't be quite so grisly if Cromwell hadn't died in 1658. He had been tried posthumously for treason, found guilty (now there's a surprise – he wasn't noticeably eloquent in his own defence) and been exhumed – from his tomb in Westminster Abbey, no less – in order for the sentence to be carried out.

'Red Lion' is according to some surveys the most popular name for pubs in England, probably because it was a common heraldic device and would have featured in the coats of arms of many a local landowner that the publican wanted to keep in with.

Saffron Hill

Saffron, a valuable medicinal and culinary plant as well as a dye, was grown here in medieval times, when the area must have been more salubrious than it was in Dickens's day. He makes it the home of Fagin's den in *Oliver Twist* and describes it as the dirtiest and most wretched place that Oliver has ever seen:

> *Covered ways and yards, which here and there diverged from the main street, disclosed little knots of houses, where drunken men and women were positively wallowing in filth; and from several of the door-ways, great ill-looking fellows were cautiously emerging, bound, to all appearance, on no very well-disposed or harmless errands.*

It's interesting to note that, after Oliver has first met the Artful Dodger, that young gentleman objects to their entering London before nightfall, so that it is nearly eleven o'clock when they reach the ISLINGTON turnpike. From there:

> *They crossed from the ANGEL into St. John's Road; struck down the small street which terminates at SADLER'S WELLS Theatre; through Exmouth Street and Coppice Row; down the little court by the side of the workhouse; across the classic ground which once bore the name of Hockley-in-the-Hole; thence into Little Saffron Hill; and so into Saffron Hill the Great.*

I mention this because it is *precisely* the route that respectable travellers from the Angel were loth to take after dark or alone, and shows that the Dodger, for all his youth, was an experienced member of the criminal fraternity.

Sicilian Avenue

This pretty little pedestrianised street off Southampton Row (see CLEVELAND STREET) was designed in 1910 as, funnily enough, a pretty little pedestrianised street, one of the first in London to have pavement cafés. The classical features of the architecture, with Ionic columns topped by a carved balustrade at either end of the street, were a deliberate attempt to add to the continental-style charm, and the name, chosen long before the average punter had heard of the Mafia, was part of the same marketing ploy.

Theobald's Road

James I (1603–25) had a bolthole in Hertfordshire called Theobalds (it's been much rebuilt since and is now a conference centre) and used to ride along this road to get there. Theobald was a common surname in medieval times and meant 'bold people' – a name that you were likely to hang on to over the generations if it had been applied to one of your ancestors.

BLOOMSBURY AND FITZROVIA

Now inextricably associated with Virginia Woolf and her fellow artists, Bloomsbury goes back much further in time than that: the name is first recorded in the thirteenth century. By then the Old

English *burh* meaning a fortified place had evolved into Middle English *bury*, a manor. This particular manor was owned by a family of French origin called de Blémont or Blemund. In their day the area was largely open fields; it was drained by Blémont's Dyke, later called the Bloomsbury Great Ditch. The process by which Blémonts became corrupted to Blooms isn't an obvious one, but if you swallow the second syllable to produce Blems, decide that Blems isn't a word and then cast around for something similar that is a word, you more or less get there. For the arty connections of Fitzrovia, see FITZROY SQUARE.

Charlotte Street

Named after Charlotte of Mecklenburg-Strelitz (1744–1818), the wife of George III. She's the woman mentioned under BUCKINGHAM PALACE who had fifteen children, the eldest of whom was of course the Prince Regent (see REGENT STREET/REGENT'S PARK).

Cleveland Street

Charles Fitzroy, second Duke of Cleveland, first Duke of Southampton (1662–1730), was the eldest son of Charles II by the mistress known variously as Barbara Villiers, Lady Castlemaine and the Duchess of Cleveland. The king had created the title Duchess of Cleveland for Barbara and gave it the special privilege of passing through an illegitimate line. Charles Fitzroy therefore had the dual distinction of being a bastard who was allowed to inherit and of being styled 'the second Duke' when there hadn't been a first. Cleveland Street was built on land that he owned and Southampton Row was also named in his honour. See EUSTON ROAD and FITZROY SQUARE for more about this family.

Coram's Fields

In 1739 a shipmaster called Thomas Coram (c.1668–1751) petitioned for a royal charter to enable him to establish a hospital for 'the reception, maintenance, and education of exposed and deserted young children'. The petition gives a horrific indication of the situation he was trying to combat:

> *...no expedient has been found out for preventing the frequent murders of poor infants at their birth, or for suppressing the custom of exposing them to perish in the streets, or putting them out to nurses who, undertaking to bring them up for small sums, suffered them to starve, or, if permitted to live, either turned them out to beg or steal, or hired them out to persons, by whom they were trained up in that way of living, and sometimes blinded or maimed, in order to move pity, and thereby become fitter instruments of gain to their employers.*

Permission was granted and the first 'foundling' hospital was duly opened in HATTON GARDEN. Its governors, however, soon bought a site – too big for their needs, but the landlord refused to subdivide it – whose position a nineteenth-century survey later described as 'near the balmy meads of LAMB'S CONDUIT Fields, then far away out in the green pastures, five minutes' walk from HOLBORN'. Coram's governors were wise enough to understand that children needed fresh air and exercise, so they took advantage of the oversized site to lay out substantial gardens. They were also canny enough to rent out the rest of the land, the income from which did no harm to the new hospital's coffers. An early benefactor was the composer Handel, who gave an annual charitable performance of his *Messiah* on the premises, frequently raising close to the vast sum of £1,000 in a single night.

The hospital moved out of London in the 1920s and no longer exists as such, although the charitable Thomas Coram Foundation for Children, better known as Coram, carries on the good work. The gardens live on, however, as a public park known as Coram's Fields and to this day adults cannot go in unless they are accompanied by a child.

Euston Road

For the derivation of Euston itself, see the box on *Mainline Stations*, page 130. The main road that now runs past the station came into being in the early eighteenth century, fully 100 years before the railway came to town. At that time, what is now OXFORD STREET was frequently congested with animals being driven to SMITHFIELD Market and, as the area south of it (modern MAYFAIR) was becoming a smart residential area, the locals were anxious to raise the tone. (The nimbyism of these people was a powerful thing – see MARBLE ARCH for another example of their attempts to clean up the place.) A New Road was therefore created, as perhaps London's first bypass, to take the farming traffic. It became Euston Road in the 1850s, named after the station which in turn had been named after Euston Square, developed in the 1820s.

Fitzroy Square

Fitzroy means 'illegitimate offspring of the king'. Charles II had a number of children by his mistress Lady Castlemaine; for his acknowledgement of the eldest son, see CLEVELAND STREET. For the second son, Henry Fitzroy (1663–90), he created the title Duke of Grafton.

Henry's son Charles, the second Duke (1683–1757), was responsible for building the New Road which became EUSTON ROAD. It was this man's son, also Charles (1737–97), who developed Fitzroy Square and the area around it. From an early stage this was the home and/or drinking ground of artists and writers, notably the members of the Pre-Raphaelite Brotherhood and later of George Bernard Shaw, Virginia Woolf, Augustus John, Dylan Thomas and others. The name Fitzrovia was coined around 1940 in a jokey attempt to give this bohemian area the sort of kudos associated with BLOOMSBURY and BELGRAVIA.

To clear up a few more names around this area, there is a Grafton Street, a Grafton Way and a Grafton Mews, named after the family; Charles married Anne Warren, hence Warren Street; and see also TOTTENHAM COURT ROAD.

Goodge Street

Another street named after the developers, in this case a pair of brothers, Francis and William Goodge, going about their business in the mid-eighteenth century. The land had previously been known as Crab Tree Field, so must at one time have boasted an orchard.

Great Ormond Street

As we saw under CORAM'S FIELDS, this area was almost rural in the eighteenth century: Great Ormond Street itself had 'fine new buildings' in 1708, and in 1734 'that side of it next the fields' was described as being 'beyond question one of the most charming situations about town'. It is probably named after James Butler, Duke of Ormonde (1610–88), an important statesman during the reign of Charles II, but it is difficult to be sure: his town residence was in ST JAMES'S, where there is still a side street called Ormond Yard.

The Hospital for Sick Children, as it was originally called, which made this street world famous, was founded in 1852.

Lamb's Conduit Street

In the days before decent plumbing arrangements, conduits were an important means of transporting water from source (whether it be river, lake or well) to consumer. From the thirteenth century a major one ran from the Tyburn Springs in HAMPSTEAD all the way to the City, passing along what is now Conduit Street in MAYFAIR. Three hundred years later, Stow tells us, one William Lamb, 'gentleman and clothworker…built a Water Conduit at Oldborne [HOLBORN] to his charges of fifteen hundred pounds'.

If you do the sums using the Retail Price Index, that is nearly £300,000 in today's money; if you base it on average earnings it is close to £4 million. Either way, it is no wonder Stow was impressed. And, never mind the expense, the conduit was no mean achievement: 'the water was carried along in pipes of lead more than 2,000 yards [a bit over 1,800 metres]' and William had also made arrangements for the disposal of waste. And – is anybody involved in Transport for London reading this? – the work was completed in less than five months. Good on you, Will.

Lamb's wasn't the only conduit in the area, nor the most interestingly named: Strype, describing the boundary of the parish of ST GILES, says that it runs 'Northward by the Wall of the Gardens belonging to King street in BLOOMSBURY; and so streight into the Fields to the Conduit called the Devils Chimney'. According to the architectural scholar Nikolaus Pevsner (1902–83), this conduit 'served originally as an extension to the White Conduit which supplied the Grey Friar's Monastery (later Christ's Hospital, Queen's Square)'. It was dismantled and moved to ROSEBERY AVENUE in 1927, and is now a listed building.

Despite all these conduits, this was still a more or less rural area in the eighteenth century: a 1766 map marks Lamb's Conduit Fields and shows Montagu House and Bedford House (see MONTAGUE PLACE and RUSSELL SQUARE) as the northernmost points of the built-up area.

Montague Place

This is how it is spelt on modern street maps, though the first Duke of Montagu (1638–1709) tended to leave off the *e*. He was a courtier and diplomat during the reign of Charles II and built himself one of the most splendid houses in London in the then-fashionable area of BLOOMSBURY. He was able to pay for it because of the fabulous wealth of his wife, the former Duchess of Albemarle, who was also sadly (but probably conveniently) insane. *The London Encyclopaedia* tells us that 'having declared that she would marry no one but a crowned head, [she] was persuaded to believe that Montagu was the Emperor of China and, in the role of Empress, was served at Montagu House on bended knee'. When Bloomsbury ceased to be fashionable 100 years later, the family sold the house to the trustees of the newly founded British Museum for just over £10,000. The building was demolished to make way for a larger one in the 1840s, but the museum is still on the same site.

Russell Square

This is another example of members of an aristocratic family looking to make money out of land that they owned; in this case it was the Earls and later Dukes of Bedford, descendants of the earl who had been responsible for building COVENT GARDEN. You may remember that their family name is Russell. One of them married the daughter of the Earl of Southampton and through her acquired much of what is now BLOOMSBURY, though it was then open fields. Evelyn tells us that Southampton had started work on 'a noble square or Piazza, a little towne'; it was to become Bloomsbury Square. Piazza was obviously still an in word: Evelyn was writing in 1665, a generation after Inigo Jones used it in Covent Garden.

Major expansion took place in this area in the late eighteenth century: Russell Square itself was laid out by the great landscape designer Humphrey Repton in 1800. It will help you to decipher a lot of other names in the neighbourhood if you know that the Bedfords' 'principal seat' is Woburn Abbey in Bedfordshire and the courtesy title held by the Duke's eldest son is Marquess of Tavistock. (It is not a coincidence that there are also a Bedford Street, a Russell Street, a Tavistock Street and a Southampton Street in Covent Garden.) And, to extend the family connection, the fourth Duke of Bedford married a woman rejoicing in the name of Lady Gertrude Leveson-Gower, after whom Gower Street is named. Malet Street, the home of the University of London, commemorates Sir Edward Malet, who married a daughter of the ninth duke.

One thing about the Bedfords that may cause confusion is that they originally lived in a mansion on the STRAND which backed on to Covent Garden and was known as Bedford House. When they moved to Bloomsbury that house was demolished and they took over the residence of the Earl of Southampton on the north side of Bloomsbury Square, changing its name from Southampton House to Bedford House. The fifth Duke of Bedford, something of a spendthrift, auctioned off the contents of the house in 1800: he is said to have raised a total of £6,000, including ninety-five guineas for a Raphael painting, ninety for a Gainsborough and sixty for four paintings by Cassanovi which had cost £1,000. The house, which was probably designed by a pupil of Inigo Jones, was pulled down. So, a philistine as well as a spendthrift, you might say. Anyway, it means that although there have at various times been two Bedford Houses in two distinct locations, there is now no such place.

Tottenham Court Road

A map dated 1766 shows a manor called Tottenham Court at the top of the road that now bears its name. In fact, the manor is much older than that, being listed in the Domesday Book as belonging to the Canons of St Paul's. The name was originally Tottenhale, meaning 'a nook of land belonging to a man called Totta'. A man of the same name (there's no reason to suppose it was the same man) owned the homestead in north-east London that became Tottenham; it is likely that over the years Tottenhale evolved into Tottenham because *–ham* is a more common ending than *–hale* and people comparing the two assumed that the latter must be wrong.

Totteridge in North London was previously spelt Tatteridge (and variations thereof), and means a ridge associated with a man named Tāta. The first spelling with an *o* appears in the early seventeenth century and may be another result of the uninitiated comparing two similar things and thinking they should be identical.

NORTH CAMDEN

A borough that starts out very urban extends northwards into hills and greenery.

Belsize Park

Bel assis(e) is the Norman French for 'beautifully situated' and Belsize Manor was, apparently, precisely that. Pepys visited in 1668, when it was owned by Lord Wotton and remarked that the garden was 'wonderfull fine: too good for the house the gardens are, being, indeed, the most noble that ever I saw, and brave orange and lemon trees'. In the eighteenth century the land was converted into a 'pleasure garden' where people with money to spend could hunt, listen to music and dance. Both house and garden subsequently went through various incarnations before being demolished and built over in 1854. Nowadays there isn't even a park in Belsize Park – you have to clamber up the hill to HAMPSTEAD Heath or down to PRIMROSE HILL to watch the privileged classes enjoying their privileges. But the name of the area was well enough established to be repeated in the tube station, which opened in 1907, fifty years after the manor and park ceased to be.

Pepys' Lord Wotton, by the way, was Philip Stanhope, second Earl of Chesterfield (1634–1713), the man who wrote letters to his son about having polished manners and getting on in society. At the time of Pepys' visit he had recently inherited the estates of two parents who were among the richest people in the country. So it is no wonder that his garden was impressive and he had time to fret about his son's social graces.

Chalk Farm

This area is first recorded in the thirteenth century as Chaldecote, which means 'cold cottages'. No one is quite sure why. The transformation from 'chal' to 'chalk' is an example of what the experts call 'folk etymology', otherwise known as 'the people getting it wrong'. To be fair to the folk, however, there was once a pub here called the White House: its whitewashed walls were part of the reason for the confusion.

Gospel Oak

Trees were often used in medieval times to mark boundaries and there was an oak tree here in the eighteenth century, where the parishes of HAMPSTEAD and St Pancras (see the box *Mainline Stations*, page 130) meet. 'Gospel' refers to the medieval Christian custom of 'beating the bounds', an annual event during which the people of a parish walked round its borders and literally beat certain important boundary markers. Hymns were sung, prayers offered for the protection of the parish and its parishioners and – most importantly for the name of this place – parts of the gospels read.

The church of Little St Mary's in Cambridge is one of a number across England that maintain this custom; its website explains that 'in an age when few could read, and before accurate maps were available, the annual ceremony was the most effective way to maintain awareness of the limits of the parish and pass on this knowledge to succeeding generations'.

Hampstead

Hampstead is made up of two common Old English elements: *ham*, 'homestead or estate' and *stede*, 'site of a building' or simply 'place'. So the combination of the two ends up meaning little more than 'village'. (The insertion of the *p* is a bit of a mystery: the obvious explanation is to make it easier to pronounce. But if so, why do most of us say 'Hamstead'?)

There was a settlement here in pre-Norman times, but it remained a long way from town for many centuries. Wolves roamed Hampstead Heath in the thirteenth century and highwaymen frequented it in the seventeenth.

It was still a separate village in the mid-nineteenth century – Hampstead Road, which leads to it, merits an entry in Wheatley's *London Past and Present*; Hampstead itself is too far out to concern him. It had nevertheless been in and out of fashion for a while: a well whose waters were said to have healing powers as strong as those at Tunbridge Wells was discovered around 1700 (and is still commemorated in Well Road and Well Walk, just off the heath) and attracted large numbers of visitors. Then the gentry decided that too many of those visitors were not the sort of people they wanted to mingle with and took their business elsewhere. Nevertheless, Daniel Lysons, writing about the *Environs of London* in the 1790s, waxes eloquent about its beautiful situation and tells us that 'Hampstead has been the residence of many eminent persons'; he then goes on to list a number of largely forgotten literati. But he was writing in the year Keats was born, thus eighteen years before the youthful poet moved into the village, fell in love with the girl next door and left the imprint of romantic poetry on Hampstead for ever more.

Hampstead Garden Suburb, which is actually in GOLDERS GREEN, was founded in 1907 as the brainchild of a philanthropist called Dame Henrietta Barnett (1851–1936). Inspired by the work of Ebenezer Howard in Letchworth, the world's first 'garden city', a few years earlier, Dame Henrietta wanted to create a quiet, pleasant urban environment in which people from all classes – as they phrased it in those days – could live side by side. The suburb was and is based round a central square designed by Sir Edwin Lutyens, which most people would agree was an excellent first step towards creating a pleasant urban environment.

Kentish Town

What are they talking about? It's nowhere near Kent.

No, but it seems to be connected with Kent nevertheless. Kentisston is recorded in the early thirteenth century, and the ending, as in PADDINGTON and KENSINGTON, means 'estate or farmstead'. The rest of the name does indeed mean Kentish and is probably a nickname, so that the whole thing becomes 'the estate belonging to the chap from

Kent'. It's possible that Kentiss or de Kentiss was by this time an established surname, but even if that is the case the de Kentiss family would have been so called because someone somewhere back in the family tree came from Kent.

Mornington Crescent

Non-London-based fans of *I'm Sorry, I Haven't a Clue* may be surprised to learn that a street with this name actually exists, but it does, and has done since the 1820s. There's a Mornington Place, Street and Terrace, too. They are all named after the Earl of Mornington, an Irish peer whose daughter married into the Fitzroy family (see FITZROY SQUARE). Mornington comes from a personal name, Mornán, rather than having any connection with mornings.

WHICH KING, WHICH QUEEN?

King's Cross is named after a monument to George IV (1820–30), erected in the year of his death at the corner of PENTONVILLE ROAD, Gray's Inn Road (see the box *In the Name of the Law*, page 139) and what is now EUSTON ROAD. The statue was demolished in 1845 but the name stuck to the area and was given to the railway station when it opened in 1852. There is a much-repeated and much-poo-poohed legend that the ancient British queen Boudicca is buried under the station. The site of her grave is said to be between platforms 9 and 10, suggesting, surely, that she didn't commit suicide to avoid capture after being defeated in battle, as some historians claim: she simply ran through the wall and escaped to Hogwarts.

King's Road (Kensington and Chelsea) is named after Charles II (1660–85), who used it as his private route to Hampton Court. It remained private, with access permitted only to those who had the monarch's permission to be there, until 1830.

Kingsbury (Brent) dates back to Anglo-Saxon times and means 'stronghold associated with a [long-forgotten] king'. The name of the area was given to a station on the Metropolitan Line in the 1930s; two years later, as the line was extended, a name was needed for the next station north and a newspaper competition was run to find one.

Queensbury, the winning entry, was applied first to the station, then to the area around it and refers to no particular queen. The two stations spent only a few years on the Metropolitan Line; that branch of it was taken over by the Bakerloo Line in 1939 and by the new Jubilee Line in the 1970s.

Kingsland Road (Hackney) refers not to a specific king but to land belonging to the Crown. Kingsland as the name of an area is first recorded in the late fourteenth century, but from the time of the Domesday Book 300 years earlier records across the country had been pretty clear about which land belonged to the king and therefore where he was getting his tax revenues from.

Kingsway (Camden) was laid out in 1905 and named after the reigning monarch, Edward VII (1901–10).

Queen's Gate (Kensington), **Queensway** (Westminster), **Queen's Park** (Brent), **Queen's Road** (Southwark) and **Queenstown Road** (Wandsworth) all date from the nineteenth century and are named in honour of Queen Victoria. (For more panegyrics to her, see Victoria in the box *Mainline Stations*, page 130.) Although the football team **Queen's Park Rangers** is based at SHEPHERD'S BUSH, it took its name from Queen's Park in Brent because, in the 1880s, that is where most of its players came from. So it is, indirectly, named after Queen Victoria as well.

Pentonville Road

Pentonville was a deliberately posh name for a planned suburb, built on grounds belonging to Henry Penton MP in 1774. And this is far from being the only road Henry named after himself – Penton Street, Grove and Rise can all be found within spitting distance of Pentonville Road, and there is a Penton Place south of the river near CAMBERWELL, where he also leased land for development. But the French-sounding *–ville* was calculated to make the suburb appeal to the better class of purchaser that Henry doubtless wanted to attract.

Not long after this the French Revolution and then Napoleon came along and things French rather fell from favour in England. To the west of Pentonville, Somers Town, built on land owned by Lord Somers, dates from this period, so it missed out on being called Somersville.

Primrose Hill

Although it is just across the canal and the road from REGENT'S PARK, the park known as Primrose Hill has been in existence much longer than its larger neighbour. The name is first recorded in the fifteenth century and in the sixteenth there is a reference to 'a sweet and courtly song of the flowers that grow on Primrose Hill'. So it seems safe to assume that a name that looks straightforward is indeed straightforward.

Swiss Cottage

In the early nineteenth century FINCHLEY Road was constructed as one of the main roads north and a tollgate put in at the southern end to help pay for it. Next to the tollgate, where everyone was obliged to stop, was an obvious place to build a pub. So far, so good. But that enterprising publican built it in the style of a Swiss chalet. Why? Who knows? Perhaps he was Swiss. Anyway, it was originally called the Swiss Tavern, later the Swiss Cottage, and the latter name spread to the surrounding area and the station that opened in 1868. Thus when the present pub was built it seemed logical to make it look Swiss and call it Ye Olde Swiss Cottage, despite the fact that this happened in that well-known olde period, the 1960s.

Tufnell Park

Named after its eighteenth-century landowner William Tufnell and his family, this was one of many rural areas that were subsumed as London spread remorselessly outwards in the nineteenth century. An illustration of 'the Roman Road, Tufnell Park' dated 1838 shows a church and a few scattered buildings as a backdrop to trees and fields, and although in 1848 the district boasted 'detached villas and excellent rows of houses', it was still more rural than HOLLOWAY. By the end of the century it was 'a collection of modern villas'. There isn't actually a park here: that's a bit of estate agent's licence.

ISLINGTON

If there were any logic about these things, this would be Islingdon, because it means 'hill associated with a man named Gisla' and the ending comes from the same Old English word as WIMBLEDON. But when people look at names such as PADDINGTON and KENSINGTON, and then look again at Islingdon they are tempted to think, 'That can't be right' and change it.

Islington Ponds were once a favourite place for a Sunday outing; the tea gardens were famous for their cheesecakes and custards. Pepys in 1664 recalls childhood visits to the Ducking Ponds (where ducks were shot, rather than people being punished by having their head shoved under water) and afterwards having cakes and ale at the King's Head. There is still a pub called the King's Head in UPPER STREET (though it isn't the building that was there in Pepys' time) and no shortage of cakes or ale to be had on Sundays, or indeed any other day of the week.

Angel

There was a coaching inn called the Angel from the seventeenth century and a history of CLERKENWELL dated 1881 gives us this charming touch of local colour:

The Angel Inn formerly was noted as being a halting-place for travellers approaching London from the north; who, if they arrived after nightfall, generally waited here till the morrow for fear of the thieves who infested the road beyond leading to the Metropolis, and who robbed with impunity, and sometimes murdered those who had the temerity to proceed on their journey. Persons having to cross the fields to Clerkenwell usually went in a body for mutual protection; and it was customary at the Angel to ring a bell to summon the party together before starting.

The inn is no longer there, but it clearly did good business in its time. See SAFFRON HILL for a criminal's attitude to the same journey.

Archway

What is now Archway Road was built in the early nineteenth century as a cutting through HIGHGATE Hill after an attempt to build a tunnel ended in ignominious collapse. An ancient road ran across the top of the hill, so the Prince Regent's architect John Nash (see MARBLE ARCH and REGENT STREET) designed a Roman-style viaduct to accommodate it. An anonymous painting dating from about 1820 shows horse-drawn vehicles (which would have paid sixpence for the privilege) travelling along an entirely rural road, now the A1, with Nash's impressively high central arch in the background. The present cast-iron arch replaced this in 1897.

Arsenal

What became known as WOOLWICH Arsenal football club was founded in 1886 by workers at the Royal Arsenal in Woolwich. The team moved to HIGHBURY in 1913 and dropped the 'Woolwich' from its name a year later. Yet the surrounding area and its tube station are still named after a munitions factory some 13 kilometres away as the crow flies and on the other side of the river to boot. Extraordinary, when you think how parochial most football-team loyalty is.

Barnsbury

–bury is the standard medieval ending meaning a manor (see BLOOMS-BURY), and in the thirteenth century this one belonged to the de Berners family, whose name indicates that they were of Norman origin and therefore part of the ruling, manor-owning class of the period.

Caledonian Road

The road was named after the Royal Caledonian Asylum established to support and educate the children of Scottish servicemen who had been killed or disabled in the service of their country, or the children of poor Scots living in London. The asylum had begun life in HATTON GARDEN in 1815, the year of the battle of Waterloo, in which hundreds of men from the Highland regiments had been killed, as had many from the Lowlands serving in English regiments. It expanded into larger premises in Islington in 1828 and, like the Foundling Hospital at CORAM'S FIELDS, eventually moved out of town altogether, leaving its name indelibly marked on the area it had occupied for some seventy-five years.

Before the arrival of the Scottish orphans, the area, still quite rural, was called Copenhagen Fields, after an inn called the Copenhagen House. This had probably been opened or renamed by a patriotic Dane at the time when the King of Denmark was visiting his sister's husband James I in the early seventeenth century. Copenhagen Street, off Caledonian Road, still marks the spot.

Canonbury

Another manor (see BARNSBURY), this belonged in the thirteenth century to the prior and convent of St Bartholomew in SMITHFIELD, and canons would have been among the several different kinds of ecclesiastics who lived here. Over to the west, in the borough of BRENT, Brondesbury may also have been called after a canon – it was certainly after someone called Brand, and a man of that name was Canon of St Paul's at around the right time (1200 or so).

Clerkenwell

The so-called 'clerks' or clerics' well', from which Clerkenwell derives, was one of a number that supplied the villages to the north of London with clean water in the twelfth century. The clerks who gave the area its name were associated with the Priory of St John of Jerusalem, established here by the Knights of St John at the time of the Crusades. The Knights of St John was another name for the Knights Hospitaller mentioned in the box *In the Name of the Law*, page 139. There is still a St John's Street running down from the ANGEL to the edge of the City; off it are St John's Lane and a sixteenth-century gatehouse that is all that remains of the priory.

For another medieval clerical presence in the area, see the Carthusians in the box on *The Friars*, page 25.

Finsbury/Highbury

Two more manors dating from the thirteenth and fourteenth centuries (see BARNSBURY and CANONBURY for others), the first the property of a man named Finn, the second named because it sat on high ground. The original Finsbury manor was the area now commemorated in Finsbury Circus and Finsbury Square, near MOORGATE. Finsbury Park was built in the 1860s on the site of the former Hornsey Wood, which was cut down to make room. Its name and location provoked this angry cry in an 1877 *Handbook to the Environs of London*:

> *[Finsbury Park] is a foolish misnomer. The site has always been known as Hornsey Wood; Finsbury lies miles away, with HOLLOWAY, HIGH-BURY, ISLINGTON and Hoxton intervening; and it tends to the confusion of local tradition, historical records, and topographical accuracy thus to obliterate, or transfer and confound local names of well-defined and long-standing usage.*

Another account of the same period remarks, more temperately, 'It ought to be styled, in common honesty, Hornsey Park.' The reason for the name seems to be that, at a time when London was becoming increasingly crowded and the poor were living in the conditions so often deplored by Dickens, the park was created to provide the residents of Finsbury with some open space.

Highgate

It was once common practice for the owner of the land over which a major road ran to set up a tollgate and charge travellers for the privilege of passing through. (Where is the Ramblers' Association when you need it? Answer: not established until 1931, about 600 years too late for our purposes.) So the gate here was a tollgate, called 'high' for the simple reason that it was on the hill that now bears its name.

Holloway Road

There is a lot of high ground in North London, as names such as HIGHBURY and HIGHGATE will attest. Holloway Road runs through a low bit – it is, simply, a way through a hollow.

Old Street

'Street' in old names often refers to a Roman road, or at least a paved one, as opposed to the more common dirt tracks, and this is a case in point. Stow describes it as 'the old highway from Aldersgate for the north-east parts of England, before Bishopsgate was built'; certainly it is recorded as 'old' by the end of the twelfth century.

Rosebery Avenue

The Earl of Rosebery (1847–1929), former Foreign Secretary and future Prime Minister, was the first chairman of the London County Council when it was set up in 1889 and this road, running through the old Fleet valley (see FLEET STREET), was constructed under his jurisdiction. Until shortly before this time the aptly named Coldbath Fields Prison had been located towards the southern end of the new road (there had once been a cold spring there, but it wasn't as popular as the warmer water coming out of the ground at CLERKENWELL and ISLINGTON). When this was demolished it was replaced by the post office sorting office known as Mount Pleasant. *The London Encyclopaedia* suggests that this name was ironic: in Strype's day the area boasted (if that is the word) a bear garden where bear- and bull-baiting took place. Strype describes it as 'a dirty Place, with some ill Buildings'. Nevertheless the name, impervious to irony, survives to this day.

Sadler's Wells

I like the sound of Richard Sadler. He discovered a well on his property, announced to the world that it produced health-giving waters, opened a 'music house' on the site and – this to me is the stroke of genius – charged people threepence to drink the water, then threw in the entertainment for nothing. Islington was at this time (1683) a village a good couple of kilometres out of town, but people flocked. One commentator remarked that the waters 'do you neither good nor harm, provided you don't take too much of them', but nobody else seemed to care.

Fashions come and go, though, and by the early eighteenth century Sadler's Wells' entertainment and clientele had both drifted substantially down market. Revivals and subsequent declines have followed ever since – the present theatre (showing no signs of decline, I hasten to add) is the sixth on the site to have borne the name of the enterprising founder of the first one.

Upper Street

Any pedant will tell you that comparatives can't stand alone, so that where there is an Upper there ought to be a Lower. And so it once was in Islington. The road running northwards, up the hill, from the present ANGEL tube station was and still is Upper Street; the one veering off to the north east was Lower Street. Its name was later changed to Essex Road, because if you keep going along it you will eventually end up in Essex. You have to do a sharp right in Ball's Pond Road, but from there on it is pretty plain sailing. And, because that remark raises another question, Mr Ball seems to have been a publican here during the reign of Charles II (1660–85). He owned one of the ducking ponds (mentioned in the introduction to this section, page 159) that first made the area popular.

SOUTH OF THE RIVER
SOUTHWARK, LAMBETH AND WANDSWORTH

After coming to terms with the invading Vikings and giving them the northern part of England to keep them happy (see the Introduction, page 4), Alfred the Great set about organising and fortifying the rest of his kingdom. One of the first places he had to protect was SOUTH-WARK, just across London Bridge and therefore an important strategic site when it came to protecting the southern approaches to the City. The land to the west of this was largely marsh. Flat, difficult to defend and likely to give you malaria: you can see why it wasn't popular. The land dried out gradually over the centuries, but wasn't properly drained until the eighteenth; LAMBETH Palace, official residence of the Archbishop of Canterbury, was built on a dry patch from about 1200, but the ecclesiastical dignitaries generally came and went by boat.

SOUTHWARK

The first part of Southwark's name is self-explanatory; the second comes from the ancestor of the modern 'work' or 'earthwork' – basically another word for fortification. After the Norman Conquest, Southwark earned a reputation for riotous living: with a curfew in force in the City from 9 p.m. (see Bow Lane), an area where that rule didn't apply became a magnet for theatres, whores and after-hours drinking.

Bermondsey

Other names in this chapter indicate that this low-lying part of town was once a marsh, and the ending of Bermondsey tells us that it was a patch of dry land in the middle of the damp. The rest of it means that it was associated, in Anglo-Saxon times, with a man called Beorn-mund. Who he? As so often (see, for example, Paddington and Putney), we don't know.

Borough

Although the name ultimately derives from the Old English *burh*, 'a fortified place' (see the Introduction, page 4), in this context is short for 'the Borough of Southwark'. In contrast to places such as Knights-bridge and Kensington, which were for many centuries isolated settlements, the name of Borough indicates that it was a part of London that just happened to lie outside the City walls.

Camberwell

The ancient well that gave Camberwell its name was discovered in a private garden in 2009; a local historian had pinpointed the location using nineteenth-century Ordnance Survey maps. The well is at least 2,000 years old and seems to have provided clean water to people for several kilometres around. There are various explanations of the *camber* part. One, that it is associated with the Latin *camera*, meaning a room and referring to some sort of structure over the well. Wells were often considered holy in pre-Christian times, so this has a ring of truth

– there could easily have been a shrine to a pagan god. Alternativiely, it may be related to *camber*, meaning the arch in the surface of a road and thus extended to people – the crippled or 'arched of body' who were cured by the well's healing waters. Less probable, you might think, but the French *cambré* from which *camber* derives has something close to this sense. Finally, you could go for the suggestion that Camber was the son of the Trojan prince Brutus who founded Britain. But as Geoffrey of Monmouth, who tells us most of what we know about Camber, would have us believe that he gave his name to Cymru and all things Cambrian, it seems unlikely that he found his way to South London as well.

Perhaps the most honest approach is that of the eighteenth-century commentator who remarked, 'I can find nothing satisfactory with respect to its etymology.'

Canada Water

In the days when London's dockland was an important centre for shipping, Canada Dock dealt mostly with ships from Canada. There was also a Russia Dock and a Greenland Dock, the latter specialising in whaling ships. More recently the name Canada Water was transferred to the freshwater lake and wildlife refuge that was developed from the old dock. From this came the name of the tube station (opened in 1999 when the Jubilee Line was extended to serve the Millennium Dome), which is also increasingly applied to the surrounding area.

Crucifix Lane

A nineteenth-century survey of *Old and New London* tells us that 'not far from Bankside there was a Crucifix Lane, near Barnaby (now Bermondsey) Street and Parish Street, which, with Cardinal's Hat

Court, seem to have been so named as belonging at some distant period to the old religious house of St Mary Overies'. St Mary Overie (whose name means 'over the river') was the precursor of Southwark Cathedral. There has been a church on the site for at least 1,400 years and it is likely that it was a place of worship in pre-Christian times. It's evocative, therefore, that today Crucifix Lane should run into Druid Street.

The Cut

The area around Waterloo Station developed rapidly with the arrival of the railways and a new road was *cut* through to join Waterloo Road to Blackfriars Road. It was at first called the New Cut but, unlike many places that have been called new this or that for hundreds of years, it dropped that part of its name when the novelty wore off.

For some years the New Cut held a seven-days-a-week market to rival PETTICOAT LANE, deeply shocking a Scotsman visiting London in 1874. Strolling through the area on a Sunday, he recorded:

> *...the thoroughfare is thronged with women having their aprons full of provisions. The manner in which these untidy dames patronise the ginger-beer stalls indicates pretty plainly the dealings they had with the publican on the previous evening; and if that is not enough, a glance at the many bruised and blackened faces will show, certainly not the joys, but the buffetings of matrimonial life. Were such characters to show their figures in any town in Scotland on a 'Sabbath' morning, loaded with articles for the dinner-table, they would cause as much consternation as if a legion of Satanic forces were let loose, and the people, in their deep-rooted regard for the day, would compel these wanton Sunday desecrators to beat a speedy retreat from public indignation.*

Interesting that the fact that their husbands beat them should be counted among the women's sins; and also just as well that this poor Scotsman isn't around to fight his way through COVENT GARDEN or CAMDEN market on an average twenty-first-century Sunday.

Denmark Hill

This area used to be called Dulwich Hill – reasonably enough, as it is hilly and not far from DULWICH. The change of name came about some time after 1683, when Prince George of Denmark married the future Queen Anne: His Highness is said to have had a hunting lodge here.

Dulwich

In medieval times, when healing plants were part of every home medicine chest, sites where they grew were sufficiently important to feature in place names. So it is with Dulwich. The ending doesn't mean it was a trading post or specialist farm (see GREENWICH); it derives from a less common Old English word meaning a marshy area. Dulwich, therefore, was a marshy place where dill grew: good to know if you wanted to calm your digestion or indeed, some say, to fend off witchcraft.

Elephant and Castle

The Cutlers' (knife-makers') Hall near St Paul's has a sign outside depicting an elephant with a castle on its back. The rug on which the castle sits bears a pair of crossed swords. The Cutlers, who made swords and other weaponry as well as knives, are one of the oldest of London's Worshipful Companies, granted a charter by Henry V in 1416 (their website speculates that this may have been by way of thanks for arms supplied for the Battle of Agincourt the previous year). The high end of their range used ivory for handles and general adornment, so, sadly, they probably worked their way through a lot of elephants. As for the castle, the suggestion is that it was to indicate to the medieval public, less well travelled and less exposed to wildlife documentaries than most of us today, just how large this ivory-bearing beast was. Elephants in medieval heraldry were often shown with castles on their back and you can still find 'castle' chess pieces in which the castle is carved on top of an elephant.

So much for the symbolism: what about the place? Well, in the eighteenth century there was an inn called the Elephant and Castle in the area that now bears its name; there were probably cutlers in the vicinity at the time. A statue of an elephant with a castle on its back can still be seen outside the local shopping centre and if you think it is a bit tacky, just imagine what it looked like when the whole shopping centre was – as it was for many years – painted shocking pink.

For some reason an urban myth sprang up that 'Elephant and Castle' was a corruption of 'Infanta of Castile', after a Spanish princess who was once engaged to Charles I. But there seems to be no truth in this idea: it arose, presumably, because it seemed improbable that a name as off the wall as Elephant and Castle should have derived from, oooh, let me see, an elephant and a castle.

The Festival Hall

If you have read the entry on EXHIBITION ROAD, you'll know all about the Great Exhibition of 1851. The Festival of Britain was held in 1951, partly as a celebration of the centenary of its great predecessor and partly in an attempt to lighten the post-war-austerity gloom that pervaded the nation. The main exhibition site was the Festival Hall, built for the purpose. Not everyone's favourite piece of architecture, it has at least not burnt down, which is more than can be said for the more romantic-sounding CRYSTAL PALACE.

Honor Oak

It was Elizabeth I who did the honours here: she apparently dined under the huge tree that thereafter became known as the Oak of Honor (it's an early English spelling rather than an American one). The oak stood in solitary splendour at the top of what is still called One Tree Hill; it was struck by lightning in the late nineteenth century, but even the tree planted to replace it has been there over 100 years.

Like many ancient trees the Oak of Honor once marked a boundary; its site is still very close to the border between the boroughs of SOUTHWARK and LEWISHAM.

Jamaica Road

Pepys visited a Jamaica House 'over the water' in 1667 and the Jamaica House and Tea Gardens in BERMONDSEY are marked on a map that dates from the 1790s. This 'house' or inn is the source of the name of the road and in turn takes its name from the fact that it was frequented by people connected with trade with Jamaica. Not surprisingly, it had a reputation for selling the best rum in London.

Lower Marsh/Upper Marsh

Much of LAMBETH was once marshland, used as a royal hunting ground for the extermination of wildfowl, with the drier parts cultivated as vegetable or flower gardens. Roads across it took the form of planks and bridges laid over the bog, or gravel tracks across the higher and drier bits. The area was drained in the eighteenth century, though not all of it very thoroughly: a nineteenth-century commentator observes that the site of St John's Church in Waterloo Road (built 1823–4) 'having been a swamp and horse-pond, an artificial foundation of piles had to be formed before any portion of the superstructure could be raised'. The streets now called Lower Marsh and Upper Marsh run across the middle of where the marsh used to be, while Upper Ground marks a piece of high ground towards its northern edge.

Marshalsea Road

Anyone who has read or seen Dickens' *Little Dorrit* will be familiar with the Marshalsea, the debtors' prison in which our heroine spent the early years of her life and which gave its name to this road. Dickens' father – a good-natured improvident said to have been the model for Mr Micawber in *David Copperfield* – was also imprisoned here. The prison, once second in importance only to the Tower, took its name from the nearby Marshals' Court, which had jurisdiction over the king's household. The ending *–sea* is nothing to do with the island of BERMONDSEY or the landing place of CHELSEA: instead it means 'the office or position of…' The concept and pronunciation survive in modern English, though the spelling is now usually *–cy*, as in the little-used *marshalcy* but also as in commoner words such as *presidency* or *papacy*.

Newington Butts/Newington Causeway

Newington means 'new farmstead or estate', although this one has been around since about 1200, so is not as new as all that. The reference to 'butts' indicates that it was a place where archery was practised. The timing is interesting: according to Wheatley, the name is first recorded in 1558, the year Elizabeth I came to the throne, and 'is evidently due to the butts set up here by royal mandate for the practice of archery by the inhabitants of this side of the Thames'. Archery had been immensely important in English warfare a century or so earlier: it had won us the Battle of Agincourt in 1415, and as late as 1511 Henry VIII passed a decree that every man under the age of forty should own a bow and arrows and know how to use them. But by the time Elizabeth became Queen, firearms were rendering bows and arrows obsolete as weapons of war: when the Spanish Armada came along in 1588, English soldiers with guns outnumbered archers by two to one. At the same time, societies dedicated to the preservation of the art and to amateur competition were springing up all over the place. We know that the queen was a keen and capable archer, so perhaps she was encouraging enthusiasts of the sport. Or hedging her bets on the warfare front, in case guns didn't catch on.

Newington Causeway is a further indication of the one-time marshiness of much of this area: the causeway was built on the line of an old Roman road, raised above the damp patches on either side.

Nunhead

According to *Old and New London* by Edward Walford, published in 1878, the Nun's Head had 'been an institution in the locality for above 200 years, was an object of attraction, through its tea-gardens, to worn-out citizens'. It's probably true that there was once a nunnery on the site; the added detail that the Mother Superior resisted pressure to convert to Protestantism in the time of Henry VIII and had her head stuck on a pike as a result is rubbished by the experts but remains oft-repeated for all that.

Old Kent Road

The Roman road Watling Street ran from Dover via Canterbury to London and beyond, so from a Londoner's point of view would have been 'the old road that goes to Kent' from the earliest times. Chaucer's pilgrims used it on their way to Canterbury, having spent the night before they set out at the Tabard Inn in what is now BOROUGH High Street. (Southwark was an attractive starting point for any traveller who wanted to make an early start; until the sixteenth century the drawbridge on the south side of London Bridge was drawn up every night at nine o'clock, meaning that those in the City couldn't get out until it was lowered again in the morning.)

Officially, the Old Kent Road became old when the New Kent Road was created in the 1750s, to improve access to the newly built Westminster Bridge. The two 'Kent Roads' meet at the Bricklayer's Arms roundabout, named after a succession of coaching inns on the site over the centuries. Another offshoot of the roundabout, Great Dover Street, built at the same time as New Kent Road, is a more specific reminder of where you can get to if you take this route out of town.

A note for nitpickers: although it seems illogical, or just plain incorrect, the spelling Bricklayer's, indicating that only one brickie was involved, is blazoned across the front of the inn in a surviving print dated 1880.

Peckham

This Old English name indicates that Peckham (like many others) was once a separate settlement, later subsumed into the spreading city. *Peck* is the equivalent of the modern 'peak', so this was originally a homestead on a pointed hill. The park known as Peckham Rye has nothing to do with rye the grain; it comes from an Old English word meaning a small stream, loosely connected with the modern *rill*. The street now called Peckham Rye takes its name from the park and used to be simply Rye Lane.

Rotherhithe

The Old English *hȳth* means 'landing place' and is a common feature of place names on rivers. The *Rother* part probably means that it was a landing place for cattle, which were shipped from here across the river to the meat market at SMITHFIELD. In the Middle Ages the port was called Redriff, a corruption of 'red rose', the name of a famous local tavern, and some say that Rotherhithe is a further corruption of Redriffhithe; but this is almost certainly an unnecessary complication of a straightforward derivation.

Surrey Docks

Until the 1960s, when the newly invented entity known as Greater London took over chunks of the ancient counties, Surrey stretched right up to the Thames and far enough east to encompass the dockland area. So to call the only enclosed docks on the south side of the river 'Surrey Docks' was perfectly explicit. Very substantial they were, too, covering some 115 hectares and including the Greenland Dock mentioned under CANADA WATER.

Tooley Street

St Olave's Church, Southwark, isn't there any more, but until the 1920s it was a prominent part of the landscape near London Bridge. Say St Olave quickly enough often enough, perhaps feel you are familiar enough with the saint to call him Ollie or Oolie and you eventually end up with St Tooley or just Tooley. It may sound far-fetched, but intermediary forms such as St Tules, found in the seventeenth century, are convincing evidence that it is true and that this is the origin of the name Tooley Street.

Walworth

The people who lived in these islands before the Anglo-Saxons arrived are generally known as the Britons or Celts, but in fact were a disparate group of tribes rather than a united people. The Anglo-Saxons didn't care: the single word 'foreigner' or 'serf' (interesting that the two were considered interchangeable) encompassed the lot of them. That word was *walh* (plural *walas*), hence Wales, Wallasey, Walton-on-Thames and almost any other place name in England beginning with *Wal–*, including Walworth. *Worth* (as in Tamworth, Kenilworth and others) meant an enclosed piece of farmland, so Walworth was simply the enclosed place where the Britons lived. And if the fence kept them from spreading out across the rest of London, the Anglo-Saxons were probably only too pleased.

LAMBETH

In medieval times, landing places were frequent and important along the banks of the Thames (see CHELSEA and ROTHERHITHE and remember that for centuries there were no bridges between London Bridge and KINGSTON): there was a vast amount of river traffic and it had to land somewhere. Just as docks were later named after the country with which they traded or the business they did (see CANADA WATER), so individual landing places reflected the commodities in which they specialised. Lambeth, whose ending is related to the *hithe* of Rotherhithe, was a place where lambs were landed or from which they were shipped. In the days when this name was first recorded – the eleventh century – this area was largely marshland with some dry fields, on which presumably sheep were farmed. Early commentators, finding no evidence of the sheep, preferred to derive the name from a different Old English word and say that Lambeth was in fact a *muddy* landing place, but the presence of the b in early spellings has decided recent scholars in favour of the lambs.

Apropos nothing, Daniel Lysons gives us this intriguing snippet about Lambeth: 'The earliest historical fact on record relating to Lambeth, is the death of Hardicanute, which happened there in the year 1041, whilst he was celebrating the marriage-feast of a noble Dane. He died suddenly during the entertainment, some say of poison, others of intemperance.' Whatever the reason, the death is significant, because Harthacnut, as he is now normally spelt, was the last Danish king of England; his successor was the Saxon Edward the Confessor, whose death in 1066 paved the way for the Norman Conquest and all that followed. It's also eye-catching because, if you are a new part of town wanting to make a name for yourself as a wedding venue, this is hardly the sort of publicity you want.

See ST CLEMENT DANES for an insight into why someone might have wanted to poison Harthacnut.

Acre Lane

The derivation here is similar to that of LONG ACRE, where acre means 'an area of ploughed lane'. Long before the district was built up, there would have been a lane crossing the farm land in the same straight, no-nonsense way that the road runs today.

Battersea

Another piece of dry ground in a marsh (see BERMONDSEY), this was associated with a man called Beaduric, who was here – and sensibly climbing the hill to keep his feet dry – in the seventh century.

Battersea's most famous street, Lavender Hill, also commemorates the benefit of the drier ground. It is named after the lavender that was grown in market gardens here; the area was once also famous for its asparagus and neither crop would show a profit in waterlogged soil.

The lower reaches of Battersea, however, remained soggy until the nineteenth century, when permission was given for the present park. Much of the land was submerged at every tide, so not only did the embankment have to be built to keep the Thames at bay but, just as PIMLICO had benefited from the excavation of ST KATHARINE'S DOCK twenty years earlier, so the ground level of Battersea Park was raised courtesy of a million cubic feet (close to 30,000 cubic metres) of earth liberated from the new Victoria Docks. Wheatley tells us, in shocked tones, that the total cost of creating the park was £313,000 which, when you look at what they did with £180,000 in South KENSINGTON (see EXHIBITION ROAD), was indeed a shed-load of money.

Brixton

You get more help with the derivation if you spell this *Brickston,* because the ending is not the familiar *–ton,* 'farmstead or estate', but *–ston,* 'stone'. The stone would have been the marker of a meeting place, in this case associated with a man named Beorhtsige (Brick to his friends?). Like many of the Old English names for what used to be outlying hamlets, this one is first recorded before the Domesday Book, making it almost 1,000 years old.

Clapham

As we saw in the Introduction (page 6), because of the sporadic nature of early records, it's not always easy to tell whether a place we now spell as *–ham* was originally an Old English *hām*, a homestead, or a –

hamm, an enclosed piece of land. (A *hamm* was often enclosed by a river, as in FULHAM, but it could also be any enclosed area.) And the sad truth about Clapham is that we simply don't know.

The first part, however, we can be more sure of: whether this was a homestead or an enclosed piece of land, it was near a hill. Or possibly hills. As it still is: anywhere you walk from Clapham Junction station is up.

It has often been observed, though, that Clapham Junction isn't really in Clapham, it's more like BATTERSEA. The story goes that in the 1860s the railways were expanding and a junction was needed: lines from Victoria and Waterloo (see the box on *Mainline Stations*, page 130) converged here, as they do today. But at the time Battersea was considered downmarket and the railway companies, eager to attract punters to this comparatively new means of transport, decided to ignore geography in favour of a name with more pulling power. It must have worked: a survey dated 1878 noted that 'this junction is the most busy railway station in England, and, perhaps, in the world', with 863 trains stopping and 138 passing through without stopping every day. The figures have roughly doubled since then, but Clapham Junction remains one of the busiest stations in the world. Even though it's in Battersea.

Coldharbour Lane

There have been various places called Coldharbour scattered through London over the centuries and they have one thing in common: they were cold, inhospitable places. The most likely explanation for Coldharbour Lane uses 'harbour' in the old sense of 'shelter': there was probably a roadside shelter here offering travellers protection from the weather but precious little else. Food? Beds? What do you think this is, THE RITZ? (If so, see page 80.)

Gipsy Hill

Self-explanatory: gipsies lived here for several centuries until an Act of Parliament enabled the police to move them on.

Herne Hill

The early explanation that the area was frequented by herons seems, sadly, not to be true. More likely is that the name comes from the Old English for a corner of land, or from a family living here in the seventeenth century. Nearby Tulse Hill is also named after a local family and is not, so far as I know, recorded in song as being twenty-four hours from anywhere.

Kennington

Very similar in derivation to KENSINGTON, this means 'estate associated with a man named Cēna'. Before the Oval Cricket Ground was built (see the box below), Kennington's main claim to fame was a gallows which was 'the usual place of execution for this division of the county of Surrey'; huge crowds were also attracted to fairs, boxing matches and the preaching of George Whitefield and the Wesley brothers mentioned under WORSHIP STREET. When public executions were discontinued, the church of St Mark's was built on the site of the gallows and remains there to this day.

THE HOMES OF CRICKET

Cricket has been around for so long that its major rival in the popularity stakes was once archery, but it really started to come into its own at the end of the eighteenth century.

Thomas Lord (1755–1832) seems to have combined the careers of cricketer, groundsman and entrepreneur. On behalf of what was then called the White Conduit Cricket Club, he acquired land near the present MARYLEBONE station, established a ground there and named it after himself. The club soon changed its name to the Marylebone Cricket Club – today's MCC – and became the ruling body of cricket. Their headquarters subsequently moved to REGENT'S PARK and in 1814 to their current home in ST JOHN'S WOOD, but on both occasions they took the name **Lord's Cricket Ground** with them. Although many of their functions have been taken over by the International Cricket Council and various national-level organisations, the MCC continues to own Lord's Cricket Ground and to monitor the rules and spirit of the game.

The Oval, London's second most famous cricket ground, is leased from the Duchy of Cornwall and has been the home of Surrey County Cricket since the 1840s. Before that it was a market garden of a sort-of-circular, sort-of-oval shape, which converted easily enough into a cricket pitch. Those not familiar with London or with cricket may be confused to learn that there are at least three sports grounds in the world known as the *Kensington* Oval: one in Bridgetown, Barbados, one in Adelaide, Australia, and one in Dunedin, New Zealand. The London ground is referred to by diehards as KENNINGTON Oval, after the suburb in which it is sited, although the official name has been changed any number of times in deference to various sponsors' products.

Nine Elms

Is there a tree-spotting equivalent of a twitcher? If so, they would be entitled to be over-excited by this name, as seeing nine mature elms together anywhere in England would be a rare event nowadays. Sadly, they would be disappointed in this part of South London. There was a Nine Elms Farm here in the seventeenth century and it almost certainly took its name from an existing clump of trees, but they have long since disappeared: an 1878 survey tells us that Nine Elms pier was 'so called from some lofty trees which formerly grew there, but were cut down before the South-Western Railway marked the spot for its own'. It seems very wasteful: the station that was built here lasted only ten years before being superseded by Waterloo (see the box on *Mainline Stations*, page 130) and the site became a locomotive works, but it was too late to save the elms.

Norwood

This is a corruption of 'north wood' and refers to a vast wood that used to stretch north from CROYDON. Why Northwood, up in the north west of London, which means exactly the same thing, should have retained the 'th' must be attributed to a quirk of local pronunciation.

Stockwell

A natural source of fresh water was important to rural communities in the days before it came out of a tap, which is why so many place names contain the element 'well'. This particular well or spring was situated by a tree stump, a meaning of the word *stock* that the OED shows was current from the ninth to the nineteenth century but is now obsolete.

Streatham

Put together the two common elements *street* (see OLD STREET) and *ham* and they form 'homestead by the Roman road'. The road that gave Streatham its name is part of the present A23, running from London to Brighton.

Vauxhall

An awful lot of London real estate seems to have come into the hands of men through marriage to wealthy women (see various examples around MARYLEBONE) and Vauxhall became the property of one Faulkes de Breauté in the thirteenth century when he married Margaret, widow of Baldwin de Redvers. (If you can't get a young heiress, go for a rich widow with no strings attached to her money has been the fortune-hunter's maxim since time immemorial.) Faulkes built a mansion which he called Faulkes Hall and this name has morphed, over time, into Foxhall and then Vauxhall.

Not an area anyone but bus-spotters get excited about nowadays, Vauxhall once boasted the glorious pleasure gardens known originally as New Spring Gardens but later simply as Vauxhall. According to James Boswell's *Life of Samuel Johnson*, published in 1791, only a few years after the gardens opened, they were...

> *...peculiarly adapted to the taste of the English nation; there being a mixture of curious show, gay exhibition, musick, vocal and instrumental, not too refined for the general ear, – for all which only a shilling is paid, – and though last not least, good eating and drinking for those who choose to purchase that regale.*

A 1751 gazetteer goes further:

Here are fine pavilions, shady groves, and most delightful walks, illumi-
nated by above 1000 lamps, so disposed that they all take fire together,
almost as quick as lightning, and dart such a sudden blaze as is perfectly
surprising. Here are among others, 2 curious statues of Apollo the god and
Mr Handel the master of musick; and in the centre of the area...is erected
the temple for the musicians, which is encompassed all around with hand-
some seats.

In short, the fashionable could come here (by boat from WESTMIN-
STER, accompanied – if they were trying to impress their companions
– by musicians hired for the purpose), listen to music, dance, take
romantic strolls in the alleyways and eat and drink to their heart's
content. So popular was Vauxhall that it inspired both the Tivoli
Gardens in Copenhagen and similar gardens at Pavlovsk Palace in
Russia, which were called Vokzal in their honour. And so important
were Pavlovsk and its gardens that St Petersburg to Vokzal became the
route of Russia's first railway line. Thus the most enduring memory
of wild nights of pleasure in Vauxhall is today found in the prosaic
vokzal, the Russian word for railway station.

WANDSWORTH

The ending *-worth* comes from the Old English for 'enclosure' and
Wandsworth was an enclosure belonging to a man called Waendel.
The river Wandle derives from the same source and was once a major
player in local industry; it falls 38 metres over its 19-kilometre length,
making it fast-flowing and powerful. It was driving corn mills in
Anglo-Saxon times and in the seventeenth and eighteenth centuries
boasted mills producing paper, gunpowder, silk, leather and snuff.

Balham

An old name, recorded before the time of the Domesday Book, and probably meaning 'smooth or rounded enclosure'. The original hamlet grew up where it did because it was on a major Roman road (now the A24), leading from London to Chichester.

Earlsfield

This ought to be self-explanatory, because fields hereabouts were owned by Earl Spencer in the eighteenth century. Unfortunately, the name is older than that and must refer to some earlier landowner. The word 'earl' was once used to signify any man of noble rank or a successful warrior and it is hard to pin this name down more firmly than that.

Putney

The thirteenth-century spelling Puttenhuthe makes it easier to recognise this as another landing place (see LAMBETH), in this case probably named after a man called Putta. I say probably because the Old English word *pyttel* means 'hawk', so it is just possible that Putney means 'landing place of hawks'. More likely, though, Putta or his father or grandfather was given this nickname because he kept hawks, looked after hawks for the local lord or, equally plausible, had a hawk-like nose. It makes you think: one casual teasing remark to a beaky-nosed friend and it is engraved on the maps for centuries to come.

Roehampton

Hampton, like HAMPSTEAD, is made up of two common Old English elements that combine to mean little more than 'village' or 'settlement'. The *Hampton* which in Tudor times gave its name to Hampton Court existed at the time of the Domesday Book, so when a place called Hampton grew up only a few kilometres away it became necessary to distinguish between the two. Hence the *roe*, which indicates that this was the Hampton frequented by rooks.

Tooting

Tōta was another Saxon chieftain whose only memorial is a place name (see FULHAM, KENSINGTON, PADDINGTON and many more). The name is first recorded in the seventh century, but after the Norman Conquest many former Saxon properties were confiscated and handed over to supporters of the new rulers. What is now Tooting Graveney became the property of and takes its name from the de Gravenel family, while Tooting Bec was given to the abbey of Bec-Hellouin in Normandy, where prayers were doubtless said for William the Conqueror's soul.

BEYOND THE CITY
TOWER HAMLETS AND HACKNEY

Several themes recur in this area: marshy areas that needed to be drained before they could be developed; green areas and individual hamlets that were swallowed up in urban sprawl; and woodland where the trees are long gone. Yet many of the names retain evidence of marshiness or of green and pleasant open space.

TOWER HAMLETS

This sounds like the sort of thing some bright spark might have come up with when they needed a name for a new borough in 1965. The name is an ancient one, though, referring to 'certain parishes, or hamlets, and liberties without [that is, outside] the jurisdiction of the City of London, and formerly within the liberties of the Lieu-tenant of the Tower'. The Lieutenant had, among other privileges, the right to levy taxes and to raise a militia. Most of the subdivisions of today's Tower Hamlets – LIMEHOUSE, SHADWELL, STEPNEY, WAPPING and more – once fell within his jurisdiction.

Bethnal Green
The thirteenth-century spelling Blithehale is the clue here. The ending means 'a nook of land' and is found in various spellings across the

country, from Mildenhall to Walsall to Maghull. *Blithe* may come from a personal name, or it may mean blithe in the sense of pleasant. The original 'green' at Bethnal was once an area of common land, turned into a public park in Victorian times and located approximately where Victoria Park Gardens (not to be confused with the much larger Victoria Park a short walk away) now is.

In Pepys' day Bethnal Green was obviously desirable: he describes going there for dinner and afterwards having 'a merry walk with the ladies alone in the garden; the greatest quantity of strawberries I ever saw, and good'. Mind you, anywhere that Pepys could be alone with ladies would have suited him. After that the area saw an influx of French silk-weavers and one of the first examples of industrial action in Britain: Wheatley tells us that in 1769...

> ...*the weavers of Spitalfields and Bethnal Green refused the wages offered by their employers, held meetings, formed a committee, and levied a tax on the looms still at work for the support of the unemployed.*

Held meetings? Formed a committee? The scandal of it. But it must have seemed so to the government at the time, because – admittedly after the strikers had destroyed some of the looms – a guard from the Tower was sent to arrest the ringleaders. After the ensuing struggle two of them were sentenced to death and, in due course, 'hanged at Bethnal Green in the presence of an immense crowd'. And we thought Margaret Thatcher was tough on the unions.

Blackwall

One of the earliest of London's docks, Blackwall was given its present name from at least the fourteenth century and mentioned frequently in Walter Raleigh's correspondence at the end of the sixteenth. Strype, writing some 120 years after Raleigh, describes it as 'a notable Harbour for Ships, so called, because it is a Wall of the Thames, and distinguished by the additional Term Black, from the black Shrubs which grew on it, as on Black Heath, which is opposite to it in the other Side of the River: or, perhaps, from the Bleakness of the Place and Situation.' Or even, perhaps, as others have suggested, because the wall itself – an embankment to keep the Thames from flowing into the dock – was black.

Canary Wharf

If you were paying attention in the section on CANADA WATER, you won't fall into the trap of thinking that the original wharf here traded in little yellow songbirds. Instead, it handled mostly fruit, from Gran Canaria, largest of the Canary Islands. The nearby Heron Quays was given this name much later, and does in fact refer to the herons that were and are often seen here.

Isle of Dogs

There's a persistent rumour that Tudor monarchs kept their hunting dogs here, but there seems to be no documentary evidence to support this. And indeed why should they have done so? Yes, Henry VIII, Mary I and Elizabeth I were all born at GREENWICH and spent substantial amounts of time there, but the tunnel under the Thames that would have linked them to the Isle of Dogs didn't open till almost 300 years after Elizabeth's death. So what would have happened when the mood took any of these monarchs to go hunting? You can't imagine them waiting patiently while the dogs were rowed across the river. Much more likely is the suggestion that the area was frequented by stray dogs, and that the royals kept their own dogs nearer to hand.

Despite its name, the Isle of Dogs was never exactly an island. It was and is a low-lying peninsula formed by a substantial U-bend in the Thames; in its early days it had a tendency to be marshy, so any dry bits would have seemed like islands amid the ooze.

Anyone travelling to the Isle of Dogs by tube nowadays will pass through Mudchute and may wonder how it came to be so called. The explanation is that this area was once as dank as its surrounds; it was made into dry land with earth that was going begging when MILLWALL Docks were excavated in the nineteenth century. There was, literally, a chute depositing the mud, which was sufficient of a landmark to give the place its name. As in PIMLICO and BATTERSEA, it's good to know that all that excess earth didn't go to waste.

Leyton/Leytonstone

Leyton means exactly the same as Luton – 'farmstead on the river Lea' – but both must have been subject to local variations in pronunciation. *Lea* itself probably means 'bright river'; alternatively it may indicate that the river was once dedicated to the Celtic god Lug or Lugh, a multi-talented personality often likened to the Roman god Mercury.

The name Leytonstone is first recorded in the fourteenth century, some 300 years after Leyton, and means 'the part of Leyton that is next to the stone'. The stone was, according to tradition, a milestone on the Roman road leading out to Epping Forest (now the High Road Leytonstone, part of the A11).

Limehouse

Lime, like charcoal and osiers (see COLDHARBOUR LANE and PIMLICO), was once an important commodity, used for fertiliser, bleaching and leather-tanning. Supplies of chalk were shipped up from Kent and turned into lime by being heated in kilns or oasts. So Limehouse comes from the Old English for 'lime oast'. The spelling Lymehouse is found in the mid-sixteenth century, suggesting that people thought 'Lymost' couldn't be right, even in the days when lime-burning was still going on. Stow uses the modern spelling, but says it is a corruption of Lime Hurst, suggesting a grove of lime trees which by his time had been cut down to build tenements for the increasing urban sprawl. There is, however, no evidence for this – well, there's plenty of evidence of urban sprawl, but none of lime trees.

As further proof of the significance of lime, there is still a Lime-burner Lane off FARRINGDON Street and a Lime Street in the City, off LEADENHALL Street, where lime-burning once went on.

Mile End

Start from Aldgate, the easternmost gate of the old City (see the box *The City Gates*, page 37), walk for a mile (1.6 kilometres) and at the *end* of that *mile* you will find yourself in *Mile End*. There was a hamlet here by the thirteenth century.

Millwall

The wall in this name is a river wall, protecting the low-lying ISLE OF DOGS from encroachment by the Thames. There were mills here in the seventeenth and eighteenth centuries, but they were removed when the area was given over to ship-building in the nineteenth.

Poplar

Strype quotes the 'Rev. Mr Josiah Woodward, late Minister of Poplar, deceased' as having provided this information:

Popler or Poplar, is so called from the Multitude of Poplar Trees (which love a moist Soil) growing there in former Times. And there be yet remaining in that Part of the Hamlet which bordereth upon LIMEHOUSE, many old Bodies of large Poplars standing, as Testimonials of the Truth of that Etymology.

The 'yet', of course, refers to Strype's time, 1720, but no one seems to be sure when the 'former times' were. The name is first recorded in the fourteenth century, so presumably the poplars were around then: calling a settlement 'the place by the poplar trees' is useful only as long as the trees are in evidence.

St Katharine's Dock

The docks were built in the early nineteenth century (and the debris used to shore up PIMLICO), but the name goes back to a twelfth-century refuge for the poor known as St Katharine's Hospital. It seems to have been the pet project of a succession of queens: Wheatley tells us that it was…

…founded in 1148 by Matilda, wife of King Stephen, augmented 1273 by Eleanor, widow of Henry III, refounded by Eleanor, Queen of Edward I, and enlarged by Philippa, Queen of Edward III. The hospital was, by the founders, placed under the especial patronage and jurisdiction of the Queens Consort of England, and has so in a measure remained to the present day [the 1890s].

The hospital was moved from the vicinity of the Tower to REGENT'S PARK in 1825 and then in 1948 to LIMEHOUSE where, as the Royal Foundation of St Katharine, it continues to this day as a charitable conference, accommodation and retreat centre.

St Katharine – nowadays more usually spelt Catherine – was the one who was condemned to death by being turned round and round on a 'breaking wheel', which is why the firework that spins round and round is called a Catherine wheel.

Shadwell

This comes from the Old English for 'shallow spring or stream'; although one early spelling is *Shadewell* there seems to be no connection to shade or shadows.

Stepney

Way way back in the mists of time this was Stybbanhythe. *Hythe* means a landing place, as you will know if you have read about CHELSEA or LAMBETH. The origins of the first part of this name, however, are more open to debate. It could be a personal name – but it would have been something like Stybba; there is no evidence for the view that it is a corruption of Stephen. Alternatively, it could be derived from the Old English for 'stump' or 'pile' and describe the way the landing place was constructed. In either case, the existence of a landing place tells us that Stepney was known for some form of commercial activity as early as the eleventh century.

It must have been important in the thirteenth century, too, as Stow tells us that in about 1300 Edward I held a Parliament here, at the home of the Mayor of London. In the course of this Parliament, among other things, 'the transporting of sterling money was forbidden'. This was the period when the King's Exchequer set up mints around the country and for the first time kept a tight check on the quality of coins produced (they also invented the halfpenny, the farthing and the groat). Stow and a number of his contemporaries spell *sterling* 'starling' and Stow suggests that the origin of the term may be 'a Bird called a Stare or starling stamped in the circumference' of the coins. Modern dictionaries don't hold with this theory, though they admit it's possible that the coins were stamped with a star.

Going back to Stepney, it had moved down in the world by the time Charles Dickens wandered through on a 'drizzling November day' in the 1850s: he saw…

> …a squalid maze of streets, courts, and alleys of miserable houses let out in single rooms. A wilderness of dirt, rags, and hunger. A mud-desert, chiefly inhabited by a tribe from whom employment has departed, or to whom it comes but fitfully and rarely.

A far cry from its medieval heyday.

Wapping

The *–ing* here is the same 'associated with' that we find in PADDING-TON, KENSINGTON and elsewhere. Wapping may have been associated with a man called Wæppa or with a marsh. Stow calls it Wapping in the Woze, a *woze* or *ooze* being a marshy place, suggesting either that he favoured the Wæppa option or that he simply didn't know what the name meant.

There was no ambiguity about the naming of nearby Execution Dock. This was the place where pirates were hanged – conveniently close to where many of them are likely to have been arrested – 'at the low water mark there to remain, till three tides had overflowed them'. Stow omits to tell us what happened to the bodies after that, but it can't have been pretty.

THE BOOK OF LONDON PLACE NAMES

Whitechapel

A name that can be taken literally: in the thirteenth century there was indeed a white chapel here. The fourteenth-century building which replaced it remained the parish church of St Mary until it was bombed during the Second World War.

Further explanation for the name lies in the fact that in the thirteenth century most buildings were made of earth with a wooden frame. The whitewash or white stone of a more substantial structure was a landmark that enabled an early traveller to identify an unfamiliar place.

HACKNEY

The ending of Hackney indicates that it was an 'island' of dry ground in the middle of a marsh. The first part is less certain: it may be a personal name, or it may refer to a hook-shaped piece of land. In any case, it was established in something recognisably like the modern spelling by the end of the twelfth century. The *wick* part of Hackney Wick is recorded about thirty years later and comes from the Old English for a specialist farm or a trading post (see GREENWICH).

Several dictionaries connect this part of London with the other numerous meanings of hackney and its derivatives, including a horse-drawn carriage kept for hire and thence the London black taxi cab; *hackneyed* meaning worn out or trite; a hack meaning a horse that is kept for riding, as opposed to a hunter or a warhorse; and a hired hack, a journalist who is paid just to churn out words. Disappointingly, the Oxford English Dictionary makes no mention of this and draws all these meanings instead from an old French word for a gentle horse. That said, Hackney was definitely rural until the early nineteenth century and there were doubtless horses kept here, so you never know…

Columbia Road

Columbia Market was established in a slummy part of BETHNAL GREEN in the 1860s by a Victorian philanthropist named Baroness Burdett-Coutts – Angela to her friends. Eager to smarten up the area and get people off the streets, she lavished a fortune on a Gothic hall with granite shafts alleged to be twice the height of Salisbury Cathedral. Overawed or perhaps just plain ungrateful, the locals preferred to conduct their business in the open air and the market never quite took off. After various changes in administration – including an Act of Parliament changing market day from Saturday to Sunday to accommodate its many Jewish traders – the buildings were demolished in 1958. By this time, however, the (outdoor) flower market was well established and remains so to this day.

So where did the Columbia come from? Well, unclear, but Angela, a fabulously wealthy woman descended from the founder of Coutts Bank, carried her philanthropy to all corners of the British Empire: she endowed, among other things, the first permanent Church of England bishopric in British Columbia. 'Columbia', derived from Christopher Columbus, is an old-fashioned, patriotic personification of America, in much the same way as Britannia is of Britain, and in 1858 Queen Victoria chose to call her westernmost Canadian holdings 'British Columbia' to distinguish them from any of that independent lot south of the border. As this was only a few years before Angela obtained permission to build Columbia Market, it may simply be that the name was fashionable, on her mind and, like OLYMPIA a couple of decades later, sounded suitably imposing.

Not one to do things by halves and still eager to improve the lot of the poor, who at the time had limited access to clean water, Angela erected a drinking fountain in nearby Victoria Park (no prizes for guessing who that is named after – see the box on *Mainline Stations*, page 130). It is some 30 metres high, made of pink marble, granite and stone and decorated with clock faces and cherubs. It is now Grade II listed – not something that can be said about many drinking fountains.

Curtain Road

The Globe and the Rose on the South Bank may have earned more enduring fame, but London's first theatres were in SHOREDITCH. The first, known simply as the Theatre, opened in 1576 and was demolished in 1598, its timbers being transferred over the river and used to build the Globe. The second was called the Curtain and probably also opened in 1576. It lasted a little longer than its older sister, but even so had descended to being a venue for prize-fights by the 1620s and was destroyed in the Great Fire of 1666.

But hold on, anyone who has been to the reconstruction of Shakespeare's Globe will be saying at this moment, Elizabethan theatres didn't have curtains. Well spotted: indeed, they didn't. The name is nothing to do with the theatre. Rather, the theatre was named after an area 'commonly called the Curtayne', which suggests that it had once formed part of an outer or curtain part of the ancient LONDON WALL. The name of the road is more recent and may be inspired by either the theatre or the district.

Dalston

An Old English name, telling us that this was once a farmstead belonging to an otherwise forgotten man called Dēorlāf. Not far away, the names of Homerton and Hoxton also derive from the owners of farm-steads, though Homerton – 'belonging to Hūnburh' – tells us that the owner was a woman. This wasn't unheard of in Anglo-Saxon times: in addition to being married to an earl and famous for other things too, Lady Godiva was a major landowner in her own right, and the names of Bognor, Kenilworth and Royston all indicate that the local property owners were female.

De Beauvoir Town

This rather grand-sounding district takes it name from the family (of Channel Island origin) who leased land hereabouts to a nineteenth-century developer called William Rhodes. Interest in the area had been stimulated by the opening of the local section of the Regent's Canal in 1820 and Rhodes envisaged an elegant residential district. Somehow, however, he had omitted to read the small print on his lease, so legal toing and froing between him and the de Beauvoirs meant that the development went ahead in a piecemeal fashion. Today, only the tran-quil De Beauvoir Square gives an idea of what he had in mind – and makes you regret that he didn't get to carry out the rest of his plans.

Haggerston

Not a farmstead, this time: this name divides as Hagger–ston and therefore becomes a stone connected with a man called Haergod. The stone would have been a sizeable one, used to mark a meeting place of some sort.

Manor House

As the most cursory reading of this book will show, there were manors all over medieval London, so it is hardly surprising to find inns popping up called the Manor Tavern. The first one in this area opened around 1820 and, having been closed and opened and demolished and rebuilt over the years, became known as the Manor House in 1931. This was just in time to give its name to the tube station that opened the following year and to elicit a sigh of relief from those local residents who didn't like to admit they lived in FINSBURY PARK.

Shoreditch

Once a medieval parish, separated from CLERKENWELL by the moor that gave MOORGATE its name, Shoreditch came to prominence in Elizabethan times when London's first theatres were opened here (see CURTAIN ROAD). In those days, Shoreditch was under the jurisdiction of the City, whose authorities disapproved of these centres of sin and iniquity – hence the migration south of the river to licentious SOUTH-WARK, where the more famous Globe and Rose flourished.

But Shoreditch's history goes back further than the sixteenth century. Folk etymology connects the name with Edward IV's mistress Jane Shore, but Stow spells it Soersditch or Sewersditch and claims that he can 'prove by record' that it had been called this for more than 400 years – that is, since about 1150; he also quotes a record of 1440 with the spelling 'Shorditch'. That is several decades before Mistress Shore became notorious for her alleged promiscuity and was forced to do scantily clad penance through the streets of London. Folk etymology being what it is, however, the imagined link with Jane Shore took a firm enough hold for a pub in the district to be named after her. (It was still there at the outbreak of the Second World War, but sadly no longer.)

As to the true derivation, no one seems to be sure, but there was probably once a ditch or creek along what is now Shoreditch High

Street. It may have been associated with an Anglo-Saxon called something like Sceorfe, or may have run down to the 'shores' of the Thames, or – given Stow's alternative spelling – it may just have been a rather unpleasant drainage ditch.

Stoke Newington

As in NEWINGTON BUTTS/NEWINGTON CAUSEWAY, Newington means 'new farmstead or estate' and is quite a common feature of Anglo-Saxon place names. So when you had two of them close at hand you needed to be able to tell them apart, and the 'Stoke' was added in the thirteenth century to indicate that this was either the new farmstead or estate by the tree stumps or the one made of logs. We are told that in the fifteenth century the manor contained about 40 hectares of woodland, so if the local Saxons had cleared a patch of land to build their farmstead either explanation is possible.

Worship Street

Four elements combine in the history of this street: one, that there was a holy well or spring here, so it could have been a place of worship in pre-Christian times. The well was still there in Stow's day: he mentions it, along with CLERKENWELL, as being 'most frequented by schollers & youthes of the City in summer euenings, when they walke forth to take the aire'. Two, that a Christian priory, which took its name from the well, owned a lot of land here from the twelfth century until it fell victim to Henry VIII 400 years later; there are still a Holywell Row and a Holywell Lane just around the corner, whose names refer to the priory rather than to the well itself. Three, that a man named Worsop was a local landowner in the sixteenth century; and four, that the Methodist preacher John Wesley (1703–91) worshipped here in the eighteenth. At that time at least part of the street was called Hog Lane, so the name might have been changed out of respect for Wesley.

Those who argue in favour of this latter opinion also mention nearby Tabernacle Street, named after a temporary building constructed for another Methodist preacher, George Whitefield (1714–70). The poet Robert Southey's biography of Wesley, published in 1820, tells us that…

> …*from the temporary nature of the structure they called it a Tabernacle, in allusion to the movable place of worship of the Israelites during their journey in the wilderness; and the name being in puritanical taste became the designation of all the chapels of the Calvinistic Methodists.*

Whatever the origins, there was in the 1980s an office building in Worship Street called Holywell House. The publishing tycoon Robert Maxwell (1923–91) took over the company that was based there and promptly changed the name of the building to Maxwell House. An example of egotism not so very different from that displayed by the landlords of BLOOMSBURY and FITZROVIA, but at least they didn't make themselves ridiculous by conjuring up a connection with instant coffee.

CHELSEA AND KENSINGTON

You'd be forgiven for not guessing this, but the ending in Chelsea is related to that in ROTHERHITHE and derives from the Old English for a landing place. As we have seen, there are lots of other landing places up and down the Thames – PUTNEY and LAMBETH are two further examples.

Chelsea was a place where they landed chalk. Chalk in its various manifestations was a valuable commodity; the chalk that was landed in Chelsea was most likely used as a fertiliser. Certainly the area was farmland at the time of the Domesday Book, where it is mentioned as having woodland for sixty pigs. The etymology pre-dates (by about 1,000 years) the development of the district as an artists' colony, so those later craftsmen who wanted to work in chalk would have had to bring their materials with them.

The other half of this borough was once a separate village well outside London proper. As in PADDINGTON, the *-ington* ending means an estate associated with someone; in Kensington it was a man named Cynesige but, again as with Paddington, we know nothing about him.

Expanding from these comparatively obscure beginnings and giving its name to a palace and its substantial gardens, a high street and much else besides, Kensington was one of twenty-eight metro-politan boroughs created in 1900 as subdivisions of the then County of London. The following year it was designated a Royal Borough, commemorating the fact that the recently deceased Queen Victoria had been born at Kensington Palace, and it retained the honour when London's local government was rearranged in 1965 and the Royal Borough of Kensington and Chelsea came into being. The only other Royal Boroughs in London are KINGSTON-upon-Thames, officially 'crowned' in 1927, although its name and royal connection date back to Alfred the Great's son Edward the Elder in the tenth century; and GREENWICH, promoted to this status in 2012 at the time of Elizabeth II's Diamond Jubilee, in recognition of its many centuries of close links with royalty.

Barons Court

Opinions vary as to the precise origins of this name, but they are agreed on one thing: there was never a baron in residence here. The estate was developed at the end of the nineteenth century and the name was probably made up by analogy with nearby EARL'S COURT. According to the hierarchy of the British peerage a viscount is one down from an earl and posher than a baron, but somehow Viscount's Court doesn't trip off the tongue quite so well.

For those who care about these things, Barons Court is spelt, on the London Underground map at least, without an apostrophe, Earl's Court with. But neither the station building itself nor the exhibition centre at Earls Court uses the punctuation. Please address your complaints, on a postcard, to someone other than me.

Beauchamp Place

From the French for 'beautiful field', this name came into being in 1885, the street having previously been known as Grove Place. Legend has it that its first residents were French officers taken prisoner during the Napoleonic wars in the early nineteenth century; certainly later that century the street became famous for little shops such as patisseries and milliners with a decidedly French flavour. So perhaps the name was a marketing ploy to attract shoppers to this *comme il faut* location.

See PENTONVILLE ROAD for another example of the perceived attraction of French names.

Brompton

The hamlet of Brompton dates back to Anglo-Saxon times: its name is Old English for 'farmstead where broom grows'. Today it encompasses a roughly defined area that includes Brompton Road; the Old Brompton Road to the west of it, running down to West Brompton station; the Brompton Cemetery (opened in 1840 and now designated a Royal Park); the Brompton Oratory (opened in 1884 – the name refers to a Catholic sect rather than anything more bombastic); and the Royal Brompton Hospital. This was founded in 1840 as 'the Hospital for Consumption and Diseases of the Chest', still its speciality. Its location was apparently chosen because Brompton – low-lying and warm – was deemed a healthy place for people with consumption (tuberculosis) to be. Nowadays the locality's 'salubriousness' takes a rather different form and can probably be attributed more to the price of the property than to the purity of the air.

Cheyne Walk

William Cheyne, Viscount Newhaven, was Lord of the Manor of Chelsea during Queen Anne's reign (1702–14). The earliest of this elegant row of houses, which over the years have attracted celebrities from J M W Turner to Keith Richards, date from that time.

Cromwell Road

In the eighteenth century there was a mansion called Cromwell House near where the South Kensington museums now stand (see EXHIBITION ROAD). Wheatley tells us that associating the house with Oliver Cromwell is a 'popular myth', although there may be a connection with his son Henry. In the same area there had also been 'a noted place of resort' called Cromwell Gardens. By Wheatley's time a century or more later 'the old pewter admission ticket to these gardens' had become a collector's item, suggesting that admission to the gardens was by invitation only and the 'tickets' of invitation were elegantly and expensively inscribed. Sadly, both house and gardens were destroyed to make way for the museums and the road named by way of apology to the one-time owners.

Earl's Court

Yes, there was once an earl at Earl's Court – the Earl of Oxford, whose family name of De Vere explains one or two of the smaller street names hereabouts. The original De Vere came over with William the Conqueror in 1066 and, like many of his peers, was granted a manor by his grateful king; a descendant became the first Earl of Oxford in 1141. 'Court' in this sense meant a manor house, though doubtless the local lord dispensed a sort of rough justice here too.

The area took its name from the earl's house, which was still there when the first underground station opened in 1871. By that time the De Veres had died out and the local potentates were the Earls of Warwick and Holland (see HOLLAND PARK). The house was demolished in 1886.

And, lest there are any students of British politics out there, yes, H H Asquith, Prime Minister from 1908 to 1916, did indeed become the Earl of Oxford and Asquith when he left the House of Commons. But he had nothing to do with the earls of Earl's Court: he was merely able to take the title because it was vacant.

Exhibition Road

There had been industrial exhibitions in Paris and in various cities across England before the one sponsored by Queen Victoria's husband, Prince Albert, in 1851. But the previous ones had been predominantly of local interest; Albert wanted something on an international scale. According to the contemporary *Comprehensive History of England*:

> *It was to be a whole world of nature and art collected at the call of the queen of cities — a competition in which every country might have a place, and every variety of intellect its claim and chance of distinction. Nothing great, or beautiful, or useful, be its native home where it might; not a discovery or invention, however humble or obscure; not a candidate, however lowly his rank, but would obtain admission, and be estimated to the full amount of genuine worth. It was to be to the nineteenth what the tournament had been to the fourteenth and fifteenth centuries—a challenge at once and welcome to all comers, and to which every land could send, not its brightest dame and bravest lance, as of yore, but its best produce and happiest device for the promotion of universal happiness and brotherhood.*

In fact, the event – known as The Great Exhibition, because its official name, The Great Exhibition of the Works of Industry of all Nations, was too grandiose for anyone but Albert himself to take seriously – lived up to the prince's vision: the main exhibition hall was the CRYSTAL PALACE, subsequently moved to the suburb that now bears its name. It covered seven hectares and housed almost 14,000 exhibitors. Some 20,000 season tickets were sold in advance; in the just under six months that the exhibition was open there were over six million visitors, an average of 43,000 a day, flocking to see everything from huge pneumatic lighthouses to the Koh-i-Noor diamond, lent by the queen. Revenue from ticket sales topped £500,000, leaving a profit after all expenses of over £180,000. Which, if you calculate it using the Retail Price Index, the more conservative of the two standard methods, is close to £15 million in today's money.

So what did they do? Aha! You've guessed. They built Exhibition Road. And CROMWELL ROAD and Queen's Gate (see the box *Which King, Which Queen?*, page 155). Along these roads, for the furtherment of the knowledge and spirit of enquiry that the exhibition had sparked, they built the Victoria and Albert Museum, the Natural History Museum and the Science Museum, all of which still bring crowds flocking to South Kensington. In addition, Prince Albert had plans for a great concert hall. He died before it got underway, but the hall that bears his name was also part-financed by the proceeds of his exhibition.

Gloucester Road

When Prince William Henry, Duke of Gloucester and Edinburgh, secretly married Maria, the Countess Waldegrave, in 1766, all hell broke lose. William was a brother of King George III; Maria, despite being the widow of an earl, was a commoner, and illegitimate to boot. The king was furious, Maria was never received at court and the Royal Marriages Act was passed to prevent this sort of thing ever happening again. From then on, all descendants of George II had to seek the Sovereign's approval before marrying. The provisions of this Act, which became law in 1772, have remained substantially in force ever since: the possibility of curtailing them so that they affect only the six people closest in line to the throne is in the news as I write, 239 years later.

This controversial lady had a house in what is now Gloucester Road at the end of the eighteenth century. She lived there until she died in 1807, after which the road (previously known as Hogmire Lane) was renamed in her honour. Presumably the Kensington Turnpike Trustees, whose idea this was, didn't require Royal Consent.

Holland Park

As mentioned under EARL'S COURT, the Earls of Holland were important landowners here from the seventeenth century. The title comes from Holland in Lincolnshire, not Holland in the Netherlands. They were also at some point Earls of Warwick, which is why there is a Warwick Road and a Warwick Gardens in the vicinity. The ruins of their mansion, Holland House, can still be seen in the park, and most of the area that bears their name was once their back garden.

Kensington Gore

Nothing to do with blood, the 'gore' part of this name comes from the Old English for a triangular or wedge-shaped piece of land. If you start at KNIGHTSBRIDGE tube, go down BROMPTON ROAD and beyond to Queen's Gate (see the box *Which King, Which Queen?*, page 155), turn north until you hit HYDE PARK and then head east back to Knightsbridge, you'll have it – it is the area that now houses the museums, Imperial College and the Albert Hall (see EXHIBITION ROAD). You might think that nineteenth-century promoters would have preferred to call their development 'the Kensington Triangle', but in fact an estate called something like Gore is recorded as early as the twelfth century and the name continued in use until the early nineteenth. Today Kensington Gore refers only to a short stretch of the northern boundary of the triangle, between Knightsbridge and the Albert Hall.

Ladbroke Grove

One Richard Ladbroke owned farmland here in the seventeenth century; in the nineteenth his descendants decided that there was money to be made by developing the area. The tube station was originally called NOTTING HILL and Ladbroke Grove is really the centre of that area – it is the starting point of the famous Notting Hill Carnival, and also the site of the hill that gave the district its name.

Notting Hill

According to Charles Dickens Junior, the novelist's son, whose *Dictionary of London* was published in 1879, 'Notting Hill is a comparatively cheap district, lying between KENSAL-GREEN Cemetery and Campden-hill, and continuing the town westward from BAYSWATER to SHEPHERDS BUSH. Here a fair-sized house may be had from about £75 to £120, according to whether it approaches the western or eastern verge of the district.' That was, of course, before Hugh Grant and Julia Roberts moved in.

Long before Dickens' time, Notting Hill was a hamlet separated from London by several kilometres of open land. Nobody is sure what 'Notting' means – it could derive from the name of a long-forgotten Anglo-Saxon, like PADDINGTON and KENSINGTON. Alternatively, the *nott*– element may mean a lump or knot of land, in which case Notting Hill becomes a tautological name, developed after people had forgotten that the word Notting included an element of hilliness.

The 'gate' of Notting Hill Gate was a turnpike on what was then the main Oxford road (see OXFORD STREET).

CHANGING NAMES

There are many reasons why street names change: patriotism, social or political change, scandal or simply redevelopment: Museum Street in Bloomsbury was renamed after the opening of the British Museum, having previously been Peter Street. There used to be a Duke Street running out of Lincoln's Inn Fields (see the box *In the Name of the Law*, page 139), but in the nineteenth century it became Sardinia Street, after the Chapel of the Royal Sardinian Embassy, where Catholics quietly congregated in the days when their form of worship was illegal. One of the many Goldsmith Streets upgraded its name from Coal Yard when the more upmarket merchants moved in. More infamously, Rillington Place in NOTTING HILL was renamed Ruston Close (since demolished) after the Christie murders in the 1950s. Bizarrely, people continued to live at number 10, the scene of the crimes. Didn't they know? Didn't they care?

This list is potentially endless, but most fun are the changes that have come about from a mixture of political correctness and squeamishness.

King Edward Street near St Paul's has seen more changes than most. Now named after Edward VI (1547–53), who founded a hospital for orphans nearby, it had previously been called Stinking Lane, thanks to the preponderance of slaughterhouses in the vicinity. In Stow's day it was also known as Chick Lane (he doesn't tell us why), by Pepys' time it was the evocative if faintly distasteful Blow-bladder Street. It then reverted to the self-explanatory Butcher-Hall Lane before settling on its current form in 1843.

Hanging Sword Alley, home of Jerry Cruncher the grave robber in *A Tale of Two Cities*, lay within the precinct of the old Whitefriars monastery (see the box *The Friars* on page 25). As such it was a place of sanctuary, where all sorts of dubious characters were able to seek protection from the law (see BROAD SANCTUARY/LITTLE SANCTUARY). The hanging sword identified a house, but whether it was a public one, a bawdy one or one where fencing was taught is open to speculation. Dickens tells us laconically that 'Mr. Cruncher's apartments were not in a savoury neighbourhood'. A century earlier the street had been known (rather too candidly, some might say) as Blood Bowl Alley, after a house of ill repute where the cartoonist William Hogarth portrayed his 'idle apprentice' being robbed by a whore.

Most graphic – but also most self-explanatory – of all was **Grope C**t Lane** (yes really), in an area of the old Cripplegate Ward known as the Bordhawe, inhabited by prostitutes. The presence of members of the oldest profession is not always described so bluntly: Stow tells us that nearby **Love Lane** was 'so called of wantons'. The place called **Maiden Lane** has disappeared from Cripplegate, but the fact that one survives in SOUTHWARK, once well known for being a risqué area, suggests that nothing very maidenly was on offer here (though see MAIDEN LANE in COVENT GARDEN for an alternative explanation). The opportunity for groping was recorded in many early names across England and, in more sensitive times, frequently underwent a vowel change to avoid offence: in Oxford, the street now known as Magpie Lane, just round the corner from another Hanging Sword Alley, had been euphemised from 'Grope' to 'Grape' as early as the thirteenth century.

Olympia

Now rather overshadowed by the more recent EARL'S COURT, the Olympia exhibition centre was an impressive architectural achievement when it was built in 1885. And that is the message that its name conveys. In Ancient Greece Olympia was the site of the original Olympic Games and anything that calls itself Olympic or Olympian is letting you know that it thinks it is pretty hot.

Pavilion Road

In addition to his work in this part of town (see SLOANE SQUARE), the architect Henry Holland was employed by the Prince Regent to extend his little place in Brighton, known as the Pavilion (see REGENT STREET/REGENT'S PARK). So when he built a house for himself, it was inevitable that it should reflect some of the grandiose features he had produced for his royal patron. The grounds of Holland's house, originally called Sloane Place, contained an artificial lake and an imitation of the ruins of an ancient priory. My guess is that the people who started calling it 'the Pavilion' were winding Henry up. But the nickname took strong enough hold for the road running down from the house towards Sloane Square to be named after it.

Pont Street

Pont is the French for 'bridge' and a nineteenth-century map shows a bridge crossing the WESTBOURNE river here, so that is probably where this name comes from. The birth of Pont Street coincides with the development of swanky BELGRAVIA, so it may be that the estate agents thought 'Bridge Street' would have been too common for their target market.

Portobello Road

There is no shortage of places in London named after battles (see, for example, TRAFALGAR SQUARE and Waterloo in the box on *Mainline Stations*, page 130), but this is one of the more obscure ones. Portobelo (from the Spanish for 'beautiful port'; the spellings vary over the years) is a seaport in modern Panama; in the eighteenth century it was an important Spanish naval base. In 1739 it was also the site of a notable British victory against the Spanish during the War of the Austrian Succession. Why the British were fighting the Spanish in Panama on the subject of who should rule Austria is too complicated a question to go into here (and see VIGO STREET for another of the same). Suffice it to say that we won and everyone back home was very excited about it, including the unknown gentleman who named his farm Porto Bello in honour of the battle. Portobello Road was originally the lane leading to the farm. The famous market, originally dealing primarily in horses, has been there since the 1870s.

The mushroom sometimes spelt portobello but also portobella or portabella is, contrary to the occasional rumour, not connected to Portobello Road. Well, come on, Portobello Road market now specialises in antiques – why would you name a mushroom after it? Received wisdom is that some 1980s marketing person made up the name because it sounded good and enabled them to sell what had previously been perceived as an unglamorously large and dark mushroom that often had to be thrown away. Shame they couldn't be more categorical about how to spell it.

Royal Oak

If you had a pound for every pub in England called the Royal Oak, you would be approximately £629 better off. The name comes from the legend that Charles II, escaping from Cromwell's men after his defeat at the Battle of Worcester (1651), hid in an oak tree. There is even a tree – in Boscobel Park, near Wolverhampton – that is said to be on the very spot, although the current specimen is a replacement planted after the original one had been destroyed by trophy-hunters.

The story became immensely popular after Charles's Restoration in 1660 and many inns were named in its honour. The one that gave its name to this area and tube station isn't there any more, but its memory lingers on.

Sloane Square

Sir Hans Sloane (1660–1753) was primarily a physician but, while in Jamaica in the 1680s, began the collection of plant species that, along with his spectacular library of books and manuscripts, laid the foundations of the British Museum (see MONTAGUE PLACE). He also become Lord of the Manor of Chelsea and endowed the lovely Chelsea Physic Garden. An all-round good egg, in fact.

The square and street that bear his name were planned by the architect Henry Holland (1745–1806 – no relation to the Hollands of HOLLAND PARK), on land that was then part of the Cadogan Estate (much of it still is). The second Baron Cadogan, remembered in a square, a place, a street and various others in the immediate vicinity, had married Hans's daughter Elizabeth. Hans Place and the various other 'Hanses' just behind Harrod's are all named in honour of the father-in-law. Indeed, Holland called his development 'Hans Town' (the name persists as an electoral ward). It was some way out of town – a map of 1800 shows Sloane Street and what is now BUCKINGHAM PALACE, but not many buildings in between. As a result it had initially to combat the fashionable world's dislike of travelling any distance from MAYFAIR. In 1818 the actress and writer Mrs Inchbald moved into lodgings at Sloane Street, 'a situation to which she had always professed uncommon dislike', and Georgette Heyer, in a novel set at the same time, has a fashionable lady refer to Hans Town as a 'deplorably dowdy locality'. It wasn't until later that century, when the outlying hamlet had become first a suburb and then a recognised part of the metropolis, that it attained its current desirability.

Westbourne Grove/Westbourne Park

The Old English word *burna* meant a stream and survives in various spellings in many place names such as Bournemouth, Sherborne and Woburn. Add the fact that the Westbourne or West Bourne was the most westerly of London's rivers and you have a simple explanation for its name. Like the FLEET, the Westbourne rose on HAMPSTEAD Heath; it then flowed through KILBURN and PADDINGTON, on into HYDE PARK, where it was dammed to form the Serpentine, and finally split to enter the Thames at two points between PIMLICO and CHELSEA. In common with most of the rest of London's rivers, it became little more than a sewer; in the nineteenth century it was covered over in the interests of public health and to allow for development of the surrounding areas. It left its mark, though: there are no fewer than twelve Westbourne Crescents, Gardens, Groves, etc. in the BAYSWATER/Paddington district. You may notice that most of these are to the west of the course of the river, so their names express a double westerliness: they were to the west of the western bourne.

HAMMERSMITH
AND FULHAM

There have been local-government links between these two places (at one time two separate boroughs) off and on for well over a century, though the present London Borough of Hammersmith and Fulham came into being only in 1979.

Hammersmith is a 'what you see is what you get' name: it is a combination of 'hammer' and 'smith' or 'smithy'. From at least the thirteenth century there was a blacksmith's forge here, perhaps with the sign of a hammer outside to attract passing trade. There would have been quite a bit of it, too: Hammersmith, then as now, was a place where major roads met. If you were heading in or out of London from or to the west or south west you would pass through Hammersmith and, if your horse needed a shoe, this was the place to stop.

As for Fulham, if, having read the entries on PADDINGTON, KENSINGTON, BERMONDSEY *et al*, you are keeping a list of 'Anglo-Saxons we know nothing about except that they have places named after them', here's another. But there is a flicker of novelty about the ending of Fulham. It isn't the common *-ham*, an estate or homestead. Early records show that it was originally *-hamm*, a piece of land enclosed in a bend in the river. Look at the map: it's absolutely true. So we may not know anything about Fulla, but we do know that he and his followers chose to settle on this peninsula three-quarters surrounded by the Thames.

Goldhawk Road

What you see isn't *quite* what you get here. The road – which is an ancient one, following the line of a Roman road that began at Newgate – seems to have been called after a family called Goldhawk who owned land here in medieval times. The name does, however, mean 'gold hawk' and presumably comes from the family coat of arms. A feature of interest is that it is Old English (i.e. Anglo-Saxon) in origin, so it may be that the Goldhawks were among the few Anglo-Saxons to keep their estates after the Norman Conquest: many, many names from this period have a French-sounding element tacked on to them because the estates had been confiscated by William the Conqueror and handed over to his loyal supporters.

Parsons Green

Another name that dates back a long way, in this case to the fourteenth century, and it does indeed mean 'parson's green' – the green where the parson lived. The parsonage was demolished in 1882 but the green is still there. No source that I can find uses the apostrophe the name cries out for, but pedants among us can take comfort in the thought that we are following older English usage: the apostrophe didn't come into common use until the eighteenth century, by which time Parsons Green was well established.

Ravenscourt Park

Time to brush up on your heraldry. *Corbeau* is the French for crow or raven and the surname Corbett derives from this; it may originally have been a nickname indicating that a person had very black hair. So it was reasonable for a gentleman called Corbett to have a raven or two on his coat of arms, and equally reasonable, when he acquired a grand house with extensive grounds, for him to call it Ravenscourt Park. The gentleman concerned was Thomas Corbett, Secretary to the Admiralty in the early eighteenth century. When the estate was auctioned off after Thomas's death in 1751, it was described as 'in the finest repair, and improved with every conveniency that can be desired...the gardens elegantly laid out, and the whole calculated to give delight'.

The estate then changed hands a number of times before being sold to the Metropolitan Board of Works in 1887. They leased it to the local council, who turned the house into a library (it was destroyed during the Second World War) and the estate into a public park, which it remains to this day.

Shepherd's Bush

It's not clear whether the derivation here is a Mr Sheppard or Shepherd, or the generic shepherd-watching-his-flocks sort of shepherd. The latter is tempting, though, for two reasons. One, the area was on the rural outskirts of London for a long time, so there would have been sheep (and shepherds) here. Two, there was once a custom of pruning a hawthorn bush to form a platform that would shelter a shepherd from the elements while he watched said flocks. This was called a 'shepherd's bush' and it would have been much more use to a shepherd than to our unknown Mr Sheppard, unless, of course, he happened to be a shepherd too.

The weakness of this argument is that there seems to be no record of a specific shepherd's bush in Shepherd's Bush; given the details that often survive about hedges and trees as boundaries or landmarks, you would have thought there would be. All you can do under these circumstances is lean gently towards the explanation that seems more probable or that makes the better story.

Footnote for the pedants: despite what I said under PARSONS GREEN above and despite the fact that a recognisable form of the modern name Shepherd's Bush is recorded in the seventeenth century, it is today spelt with an apostrophe. Go figure.

White City

A 1915 description of the parish of HAMMERSMITH gives the distinct impression that the place is going to the dogs:

> *The northern area from SHEPHERD'S BUSH to WORMWOOD SCRUBS – a district of ancient forest and waste land – contains the great convict prison, an adjoining workhouse and infirmary, and the extensive grounds of the exhibition known as the Great White City. OLYMPIA is also within the south-eastern limits of the parish. These latter, which did not displace any buildings of historical interest, can be better tolerated than the intrusion of certain unwelcome manufactories which are gradually destroying the beauty of the river-bank. Since the establishment of the Waterworks in 1806 and the building of the new bridge in 1825, the beautiful houses of the Upper and Lower Malls have been gradually disappearing, and now that the huge modern suburb threatens even these survivors, the last relics of a peaceful and picturesque hamlet are seriously imperilled. We can feel some little satisfaction, however, in presenting these records before the flowing tide has quite overwhelmed them.*

In amongst the moaning, this document explains the origins of White City. A comparatively recent name (1908), it refers to the white finish on the buildings that were built for the Franco-British Exhibition (an international fest that attracted even more people than the Great Exhibition of 1851 – see EXHIBITION ROAD) and were used later the same year for the first Olympic Games to be held in London. Funnily enough, that 1915 writer was right in thinking the area was going to the dogs: left derelict after the First World War, the White City stadium became in 1927 the home of greyhound racing and remained so until it was demolished in the 1980s.

White City's other claim to fame, as all committed trivia buffs know, is that it was here – during the 1908 Olympics – that the first marathon of today's standard distance, 26 miles and 385 yards or 42.195 kilometres, was run. A marathon had always been in the region of 40–42 kilometres, but the current rather odd figure was fixed upon so that runners would finish in front of the White City royal box.

Wormwood Scrubs

On the face of it a great name; rather less appealing when you start to analyse it. Wormwood in this instance is connected not with the medicinal plant (see CAMOMILE STREET), but with a more literal interpretation of its name: in the twelfth century it seems to have been a wood infested by worms, which in those days would have meant snakes. 'Scrubs' is a later addition, meaning scrubland, an area with low-growing, stunted trees. So not an attractive place generally, even before they built a prison on it in the nineteenth century.

THE SOUTH EAST
GREENWICH AND LEWISHAM

Everything from royalty to highway robbery has left its mark on these two boroughs, including, as is often the case with place names, river crossing places, woodland and lonely heaths. In addition, in CRYSTAL PALACE, South London boasts a souvenir of one of the great architectural and cultural achievements of the Victorian era.

GREENWICH

The ending -*wich*, here meaning a trading place or harbour, comes from the Old English -*wic*, which later indicated a specialist farm and evolved into -*wick* in names such as Gatwick ('goat farm') and Keswick ('cheese farm'). *Wicks* tend to be later developers than *wiches*: the fact that Greenwich is spelt as it is tells us that it was probably in existence by the tenth century. Oh, and it was green.

It was still green in Henry VIII's time. Stow recounts a May Day morning when the king, doing what everyone else did on May Day, ventured into 'sweet meadows and green woods, there to rejoice their spirits with the beauty and savour of sweet flowers'. He rode from Greenwich to SHOOTERS HILL and was accosted by a company of yeomen dressed as Robin Hood and his men. After treating the royal party to a display of archery, the yeomen 'desired the King & Queen with their retinue to enter the green wood, where, in harbours made of boughs, and decked with flowers, they were set and served plentifully with venison and wine, by Robin Hood and his men, to their great contentment'.

Greenwich had been the site of a royal palace since the mid-fifteenth century and was very popular with the Tudors (see ISLE OF DOGS); several centuries later the meridian which made it world famous was established after an international conference in 1884. Before that any country that cared about these things tended to calculate longitude by decreeing that its own capital was at 0°, which was a nightmare for anyone wanting to sail beyond their own waters. The fact that the Royal Observatory in Greenwich won the day is proof, if proof were needed, that in those days Britannia really did rule the waves. And it would be a shame to leave this subject without a passing reference to the fact that, when it came to the vote at that 1884 conference, France abstained and continued for several decades to base its calculations on the Paris Meridian. *Plus ça change*, one might be tempted to say.

Abbey Wood

Places with 'abbey' in their name are almost always self-explanatory and this is no exception: it takes its name from Lesnes Abbey, founded in 1178, as a penance, according to legend, by one of the knights involved in the murder of Thomas Becket. Substantial ruins are still there, if you care to take a look.

Blackheath

Also self-explanatory, but you may wonder *why* it was black. Colour of the soil? Colour of the bracken? Bit of both, probably, and the fact that it was generally considered a bleak spot may have come into it too.

Bleak or not, Blackheath has seen more than its share of activity. It was on what Stow calls 'the Black Heath' that the insurgents met before they marched on London to instigate the Peasants' Revolt in 1381; here that in 1400 Henry IV met the Emperor of Constantinople who had come to ask for his help against the Turks; here that in 1540 Henry VIII came in state to meet his fourth bride, Anne of Cleves, and had pitched 'a rich cloth of gold, and divers other tents and pavilions, in the which were made fires and perfumes for her and such ladies as should receive her grace'; and here in 1660 that the Royalist army came to meet Charles II on the occasion of his restoration to the throne.

Thereafter a fair, held twice a year, was established here; the diarist John Evelyn visited it in 1683:

This was the first day, pretended for the sale of cattle, but I think, in truth, to enrich the new tavern at the bowling green, erected by Snape, his Majesty's farrier, a man full of projects. There appeared nothing but an innumerable assembly of drinking people from London, pedlars, &c.; and I suppose it is too near London to be of any great use to the country.

In 1741 a advertisement for the fair offered…

…a West of England woman 38 years of age, alive, with two heads, one above the other; having no hands, fingers, nor toes; yet can she dress or undress, knit, sew, read, sing.

For those with money to burn, there was the further enticement that 'Gentlemen and ladies may see her at their own houses if they please'.

So, bleak Blackheath may have been, black it certainly was, but it must always have been fun once you got there.

Charlton

In Anglo-Saxon times a *ceorl* (pronounced 'churl') was an independent peasant landowner. Not a rich man, but his own master. Under the Normans the *ceorls* were sucked into the feudal system and had much less freedom – hence the diminished status (and bad temper) implied by the modern words *churl* and *churlish*. The name of Charlton, however, goes back to happier times: it is recorded in the Domesday Book, before the feudal system really kicked in, and means 'farmstead belonging to the free peasants'.

Deptford

I have said elsewhere that knowing where to cross any river was an important feature of medieval life and is the reason many settlements grew up where they did. You had to be careful at Deptford, however: its name means 'deep ford', so presumably you would have been ill-advised to attempt to cross at anything other than low tide.

Kidbrooke

This should really be Kitebrook – it means 'a brook frequented by kites'. Nobody seems to have recorded much about the birds, but the place has an odd history: a nineteenth-century gazetteer tells us that it 'lost its church and parsonage through neglect', which sounds like an extraordinary piece of carelessness on the part of the parishioners. It seems to have happened some time in the fourteenth or fifteenth century and no one is sure why; but the parish and therefore the village didn't come back to life until a new church was built in 1867.

Plumstead

'Plum' is a nice, reliable element in place names: it almost always means something to do with plums. That is the case here: this is simply 'place where the plum trees grow'.

Shooters Hill

The 'shooters' were probably initially archers who practised their craft here (see GREENWICH), but the hill later became known as the hangout of highwaymen. The road that passes over the hill (now the A2, although it has been diverted to avoid the worst of the climb) has been the main road to Dover since Roman times and the slopes are steep enough to force carriages and horses to slow down, making them easy targets. Dickens in *A Tale of Two Cities* describes passengers travelling by the mail coach from London to Dover:

> *...walking up hill in the mire by the side of the mail...; not because they had the least relish for walking exercise, under the circumstances, but because the hill, and the harness, and the mud, and the mail, were all so heavy, that the horses had three times already come to a stop, besides once drawing the coach across the road, with the mutinous intent of taking it back to* BLACKHEATH.

To add to the place's fearfulness, there was a gallows at the crossroads at the bottom of the hill. Gallows were often situated at crossroads, and most authorities explain that this was so that more people would see them and be deterred from any thought of following the deceased's career path. Others believe it was because a crossroads was a place where this world met the next: siting a gallows there made things easier for the spirits of the dead, which would otherwise wander aimlessly until they reached the age at which they would have died naturally. Hmm.

Anyway, at Shooters Hill the bodies of the hanged were displayed at the top: Pepys records riding under such a corpse – 'a filthy sight it was to see how his flesh is shrunk to his bones'. I'm inclined to think that this detail adds to the 'public deterrent' theory and detracts from the 'wandering spirit' one, but do feel free to differ if you wish.

Woolwich

Like GREENWICH, this was a trading place or harbour, in this case specialising in wool. The name and function are both ancient, dating back to before the Domesday Book, but Woolwich really began to earn its place on the map when Henry VIII created a Royal Dockyard here in 1512–13. He had his flagship, modestly named the *Henry Grace à Dieu* and nicknamed equally modestly the *Great Harry*, built at Woolwich (and indeed it ended its life here, destroyed by fire forty years later). In the seventeenth century the establishment that was to become the Royal Arsenal also opened here and 200 years later came the famous football team – see ARSENAL.

LEWISHAM

Another name that pre-dates the Domesday Book, this was once the home of a man called Lēofsa. By the tenth century it was an important parish, and in the eighteenth was an attractive suburb with an impressive high street: 'Lewisham-street is more than a mile in length, which, as well as the hamlets and environs near it, are in great measure inhabited by opulent merchants and Londoners, the vicinity to the metropolis making this place a most agreeable and convenient recess,' we are told in a *Survey of Kent* dated 1797. It must have been fashionable a few centuries before that, too, because the same survey tells us that George, Duke of Clarence – brother of Edward IV and Richard III, the one who is said to have drowned in a butt of malmsey wine – had had a house there, acquired when he married Isabel Neville, daughter of Warwick the Kingmaker. Until very recently, our chronicler tells us, Isabel and George's coats of arms had been entwined in the windows of their home. They aren't there any more (if you want to see a memorial to this ill-fated couple you need to go to Tewkesbury Abbey), but it's another sign of Lewisham's former grandeur.

Brockley

Brocc was the Celtic word for a badger, whence the nickname Brock that survives to this day. Some places whose names begin with *Brock* refer to badgers; rather more of them come from the Old English and are to do with brooks. The ending *–ley* (with various alternative spellings such as *–leigh)* generally means a woodland clearing or glade, as it does in WEMBLEY, FINCHLEY and elsewhere. So Brockley was once either a woodland clearing by a brook, or one frequented by badgers. In either case, it has changed quite a lot since the name was first recorded in the twelfth century.

Catford

We may not be sure about BROCKLEY but we can be confident about Catford: it was a ford where wild cats were found. The river you could ford here was the Ravensbourne, whose name doesn't mean it was associated with ravens (well, you wouldn't expect it, with all those wild cats about). Instead it probably means 'river marking a boundary', and it may have marked the border between LEWISHAM and BROMLEY at some earlier time.

Crystal Palace

Here's a hideous example of inflation for you. The original Crystal Palace was designed for Prince Albert's Great Exhibition of 1851 (see EXHIBITION ROAD) and the innovative structure of iron and glass was preferred because the tender of £80,000 substantially undercut the best price for a brick building. When the exhibition closed, the 'palace' was moved from HYDE PARK out to SYDENHAM to form a permanent museum and exhibition and concert hall. It was up and running only three years later, at a cost of £1.5 million. Admittedly that figure includes the landscaping of about 75 hectares of ground described in the early twentieth century as 'excellently set out for recreation', but it nevertheless makes a nonsense of the forty grand they had saved by not building it in brick.

That said, the building was a phenomenal achievement, consisting of 'a long and lofty nave intersected at regular distances by three transepts, of which the central is 384 feet long, 120 feet wide and 168 feet interior height'. That's approximately 117, 37 and 51 metres respectively, for those who don't think in imperial measurements. Big. And of course the reflections in the glass panels made it look all the bigger – the six million people who visited it in Hyde Park had never seen anything like it.

Over the next eighty years the palace was the site of events as wide-ranging as Boy Scout rallies and the world's first ever cat show, but its fortunes gradually declined: it didn't help that it wasn't open on Sundays, the one day in the week that many people would have been free to visit. It finally burnt to the ground in 1936. Old, dry timber floors and high winds combined to wreck the whole thing in the space of a night. But by that time it had a football team, a railway station (actually it had two, but one of them is no more) and a mention on the front of a 157 bus, so the name of the area remains.

Hither Green

It's tempting to think of this as a faintly seductive location, associated with 'come hither' looks, or as a dithering one, flitting vaguely hither and thither. But no. It is more practical and prosaic than that. Hither Green was simply closer to LEWISHAM than Further Green. There is still a Further Green Road, running off the alluringly named Verdant Lane, but the original Hither Green has been built over and the only substantial green space is now the local cemetery.

New Cross

Not a cross so much as a crossroads, at about the point where the A2 and the A20 meet today. In the seventeenth century, when the name is first recorded, the London-to-Dover road crossed one heading to the fashionable settlement at LEWISHAM and other points south. Like many names ending in –*gate*, New Cross Gate refers to a tollgate on the main road – see TURNPIKE LANE.

Sydenham

In the early nineteenth century Sydenham was 'a genteel hamlet of LEWISHAM', known for its 'sylvan charm', the salubrity of the air and its mineral springs. All this changed with the advent of the railway and, twenty years later, of the CRYSTAL PALACE, whose name encroached on a goodly chunk of the original settlement. Sydenham suddenly became popular and built up; by 1878 it was described as 'a place of great resort'. Like CLAPHAM, it's a name in which we can't be sure whether it was originally a *hām* or a *hamm*. So this was either a homestead or an enclosure once belonging to a man called Cippa.

OUTLYING BOROUGHS
NORTH OF THE RIVER

A lot of the places that now fall within the outer boroughs of London were once in the county of Middlesex, which in the early nineteenth century was almost entirely rural. The county's population increased from 70,000 in the 1801 census to almost 800,000 in 1901 and 1.1 million in 1911, as estates were broken up for development and tracts of heathland built over. As so often, however, the place names endure, recalling a time when the principal concerns were what the land was like, who owned it and how you could get across the river.

There will be purists reading this chapter who object to its title on the grounds that in several places the Thames kinks in such a way that 'north of the river' becomes inaccurate: HOUNSLOW in particular is 'west of the river'. While this is undeniably true, it is also (like many comments made by purists) completely irrelevant. Londoners as a breed are deeply conscious of the north–south divide created by the Thames and 'west of the river' is not an expression any local would use.

Let's start in the west and zigzag our way out to the north east of Greater London.

HILLINGDON

If you happen to know that a *-don* ending is likely to mean a hill (see WIMBLEDON for more about this), you might think that Hillingdon was a tautological name. But no: the *hill* part derives from a person, so the meaning becomes 'hill associated with someone called Hilda or Hilla'.

Uxbridge

There is known to have been a bridge here the better part of 1,000 years ago. It was originally associated with a tribe called the Wixan, but that *w* sound wasn't popular with the Normans (see EALING for another example of their problems with Old English) and spellings without it occur as early as the twelfth century.

HOUNSLOW

Modern dictionaries give a somewhat surprising meaning for 'low': 'a hill, tumulus or burial mound' – archaic, we are told, except in place names. Well, Hounslow is one of those place names in which the meaning survives: it is a mound associated with a man called Hund. It's likely that such a mound would have been used as a meeting place.

Boston Manor

No one is entirely certain about this name: the Boston part probably means 'farmstead of a man called Bord', with the 'manor' having come along later – sufficiently later, indeed, to be called a 'manor' rather than a 'bury' (see GUNNERSBURY). Boston in Lincolnshire (from which Boston in Massachusetts takes its name) is said to be connected with St Botolph but, although there is a church named after him in the City, he doesn't seem to have strayed this far west.

Chiswick

Wick and *wich*, as we saw under GREENWICH, often meant a specialist farm, particularly a dairy farm. Chiswick was specifically a cheese farm. The fact that Keswick in the Lake District has the same derivation but different spelling and pronunciation is explained by local influences: the Scandinavians who once dominated the north of England were perfectly familiar with the hard *k* sound; in the south the Anglo-Saxons and later the Normans had a tendency to soften it.

Gunnersbury

This is *–bury* in the Middle English sense of a manor (see BLOOMS-BURY), but not, despite appearances, one that was defended by artillery. It was once owned by a woman called Gunnhildr or Gunhilda, whose name tells us that she was of Scandinavian origin; she may or may not have been the niece of King Canute. Lysons' account, published in the 1790s, describes this story as 'not improbable'; modern writers tend to be less charitable. The facts that (again according to Lysons) the lady was banished from these shores in 1044 and that the name is not recorded until 300 years later may add weight to the sceptics' argument.

Isleworth

Nothing to do with an island, the first part of this comes from a personal name. Like EALING, it was originally spelt with a *yogh*, which had been dropped by the thirteenth century. The *–worth* element comes from the Old English for 'enclosure' and was used for a homestead or piece of farmland surrounded by a protective fence or ditch. At some point in the eighth century or so, Mr Gīslhere was sufficiently wealthy and sufficiently protective of his property to mark it out in this way.

Osterley

Endings in –*ley* normally mean a clearing in a woodland, and this is 'a clearing with a sheepfold'. Not obvious at first glance, the *oster*–element is connected with the modern word *ewe*.

Perivale

Slip in an extra *a* and you are almost there: 'peary vale' or 'valley where pear trees grow'.

Ruislip

Rushes were a useful commodity in medieval times – they were strewn on the floor, woven into mats or thatched roofs, or dipped in animal fat to make a cheap substitute for candles. This explains why many places have some form of 'rush' in their name: it was good to know where these serviceable things grew.

Another thing that was handy to know was where you could get across a river, hence all the place names with 'ford' in them. Even handier: get across the river without getting your feet wet, because it is narrow enough to leap.

Put all that lot together and you have Ruislip: 'the place where you can jump across the river, which you'll recognise because there are rushes growing there'.

Turnham Green

The site of a battle during the English Civil War (1642), this now rather elegant area was in the eighteenth century sufficiently rural and sufficiently disreputable to be a favourite haunt of highwaymen. The name indicates a homestead on a turn in the river, and if you look at a map you'll see that the Thames does indeed turn through approximately 90 degrees and run more or less due north between ROEHAMPTON and CHISWICK, which are adjacent to Turnham Green.

EALING

An ancient name, going back about 1,500 years, to a man called something like Gilla. The *-ing* is the same indication of association that is found in PADDINGTON, KENSINGTON and many others; so this is 'the place where Gilla's family or followers lived'. The interesting thing about it is the man's name. That initial *g* was really an Old English *yogh*, a sound like the modern *y*, which didn't exist in Norman French. When the Normans took over after 1066, their language became the influential one and the *yogh* fell victim to the fact that the ruling class couldn't pronounce it. The Anglo-Saxons may have laughed behind the Normans' back, but that didn't stop Yealing becoming Ealing.

Acton

This would once have been pronounced with a long *a* (*ake-ton*), *āc* being both the Old English for *oak* and the source of the modern word. So Acton is either a farmstead where oaks grew, or one where oak timber was produced. Or, not inconceivably, both.

Hanger Lane

The first name recorded in these parts is Hanger Wood; then came Hanger Hill and finally Hanger Lane. All derive from the Old English for a steep and usually wooded slope.

HARROW

In the eighth century this was Gumeningae hergae, which translates as 'heathen shrine(s) or temple(s) of the Gumeningas tribe [probably followers of a man named Guma]'; in the pre-Christian era, Harrow was one of the most important religious centres in England. By the eleventh century, both shrine and Gumeningas were long gone and the Domesday Book name for the place is simply Herges. Over time this became first Hareways and subsequently Harrow: the modern form was in use by the time the famous school was founded in 1572.

Stanmore

The modern spelling is an error that crept in around the sixteenth century: etymologically it should be Stanmere, meaning a stony lake.

BRENT

The London Borough of Brent was created in the 1960s reshuffle mentioned in the Introduction, but the name, originally assigned to the local river, goes back fully 2,000 years. Its origins are Celtic and suggest a connection with the water goddess Brigantia, who is herself linked to the Irish St Bridget. Brentford, though today in the borough of HOUNSLOW, stands at the point where the Brent meets the Thames and where you could ford both rivers. Brent Cross is a comparatively recent coinage: it refers not to an ancient cross at a crossroads, but to the convoluted arrangement of dual carriageways near the modern shopping centre.

Dollis Hill

No one is sure where Dollis originated: early spellings suggest that it might have been associated with a family called Dalley. The *a* had changed to *o* by the early nineteenth century, leading to a brief period when it was known as Dolly's Hill, but there is no suggestion of a connection with mini-skirted young women or with children's toys. The advent of a tube station in 1909 put an end to all debate by adopting the current spelling.

Dollis Hill House was built in the early nineteenth century and took its name from the area. It was once owned by the Earl of Aberdeen, a prominent politician in the Gladstone era, and the elderly Prime Minister was a frequent guest. The house's grounds were turned into a public park shortly after Gladstone's death in 1898 and the park (in which the ruins of the house still stand) is named after him.

Harlesden

This is a prime example of a name being mumbled and simplified over the years. It should really be Harleston, as the ending means not hill (as in WILLESDEN) but homestead. The man who first owned it was called Herewulf, but sadly Herewulfston was far too much of a mouthful to survive for long.

Kensal Green

G K Chesterton's 1914 poem 'The Rolling English Drunkard' ends with the lines

For there is good news yet to hear and fine things to be seen,
Before we go to Paradise by way of Kensal Green.

It's an example of metonymy, as I'm sure you recognised; any of Chesterton's original readers would have known that 'Kensal Green' meant not the entire suburb but the cemetery that occupies a large part of it. Kensal Green was the first of seven great cemeteries created on the fringes of London's built-up area from the 1830s. (Just as those in charge would later realise that the capital's rapidly increasing population needed fresh air and green space – see FINSBURY/HIGHBURY and ALEXANDRA PALACE – so they were forced to recognise that it was now producing more dead than the old-fashioned burial grounds could deal with.)

Kensal Green cemetery was conceived as an attractive piece of landscape, with 800 trees. Wheatley, however, while praising the tastefulness of the planting, remarks that 'there is much bad taste in art exhibited in the monuments'. He singles out as most conspicuous those of 'St John Long, the quack doctor; Ducrow, the rider; Morrison, the pill-man; and George Robins, the auctioneer'. The first of these is perhaps the most remarkable, not so much for its bad taste as for the fact that it existed at all: St John Long set himself up in HARLEY STREET with no formal qualifications, claimed to be able to cure consumption by cutting people open so that the internal malady could escape through an external route, was convicted of manslaughter when a young woman failed to respond to this peculiar treatment – and yet he still has a splendid-if-you-like-that-sort-of-thing monument erected to him by his grateful patients.

Dominant though the cemetery is in the area's recent geography and history, there had been a green at Kensal long before anyone thought of putting bodies in it. The name was originally more like 'King's Holt', which derives from the Old English for 'king's wood'. No one seems sure which king, but the name is first recorded in 1253, which makes it Henry III or earlier. Probably it was land owned by the Crown and passed on from one monarch to another.

Kilburn

'Stream associated with a man named Cylla' or possibly 'stream associated with cows'. The waters from the stream, or from a nearby spring, were sufficiently distasteful to persuade people that they had medicinal value; from the seventeenth to the early nineteenth century the fashionable and the hypochondriacal flocked here as they did to HAMPSTEAD and SADLER'S WELLS.

Park Royal

The 'park' was the Royal Agricultural Showground; intended to be a permanent exhibition centre, it lasted a mere three years, from 1903 to 1905. Although the name has stuck, Park Royal now refers to little more than a tube station and an industrial estate.

Stonebridge Park

Not rocket science, this one: it is named after a stone bridge that carried the HARROW Road across the river BRENT.

Wembley

First recorded as early as the ninth century, Wembley is one of the many suburbs of London to retain its Old English name. It means

'Wemba's woodland clearing', but sadly – as so often – we don't know anything about Wemba himself. Wembley was still a tiny village in the sixteenth century; it was the arrival of the railway in the 1830s and the building of a sports stadium (opened in 1923) that really enlarged the clearing Wemba had made all those years ago.

THE ROUND BALL AND THE OVAL BALL

A number of London's sporting venues – of which perhaps the best known is WEMBLEY – take their name from the street or area in which they are situated. These streets and areas therefore become much more famous through their associations with football and rugby than they might otherwise have been. Here are four prime examples.

Stamford Bridge is a place in Yorkshire, famous as the site of a battle in 1066 in which the Saxon claimant to the throne, Harold, Earl of Wessex, defeated and killed a Norwegian contender, Harald Hardrada. Immediately afterwards he had to dash south to try to repel William the Conqueror's invasion and was defeated and killed at the Battle of Hastings. The rest, as they say, is history.

All very well, but how did it come to be the name of a football ground in west London? Answer, it has nothing to do with the place in Yorkshire. Stamford was quite a common place name in Saxon times and meant either 'stony ford' – as in the place in Yorkshire and in Stamford Brook, also in west London – or 'sandy ford' as it does here and in Stamford Hill in east London. A ford was, obviously, a natural place to cross a river and, as technology developed, was often supplemented by a bridge; the word 'bridge' was then frequently tacked on to the existing name. The modern version of this bridge carries the King's Road (see the box *Which King, Which Queen?* on page 155) over a creek in CHELSEA and in the 1870s gave its name to the spectacular new athletics stadium that was being built nearby. The stadium changed hands in 1904 and the new owners offered it to the already-in-existence FULHAM FC. After some legal and financial wrangling Fulham declined, so the owner, as the Chelsea website puts it, 'decided to build a team for a stadium, rather than the other way round'; Chelsea FC came into being.

Fulham's home ground, then and now, was **Craven Cottage**. Not perhaps everyone's first choice for the name of a football ground, but in fact this has nothing to do with cowardice. It takes its name from William, Baron Craven, who built a cottage here in 1780, on land that had earlier been a hunting ground favoured by Anne Boleyn. The cottage burnt down in 1888 and Fulham FC took over the site a few years later.

The family name of Craven derives from their home in Yorkshire and may mean a place where garlic was grown. Craven Street near CHARING CROSS and the various Cravens – Craven Road, Craven Terrace, Craven Hill Gardens, etc. – in the PADDING-TON area are all named after the same family.

The origins of **White Hart Lane** go back to Richard II (1377–99), who, for reasons too complicated to go into here, used a white hart or stag as his official emblem. Coincidentally, he also enacted a law insisting that ale houses display a sign that would identify them to the official ale taster. Consequently, a great many pubs, suddenly needing a name, came up with the syco-phantic idea of calling themselves the White Hart. One such was in Tottenham (see TOTTENHAM COURT ROAD), long before Tottenham Hotspur FC was thought of; it gave its name to the lane on which it stood, which in turn gave its name to the foot-ball ground built for Spurs in the early twentieth century. See also COCKSPUR STREET.

As for the home of rugby union, you win some, you lose some. The origins of many place names ending in –*ham* suffer from the ambiguity mentioned under CLAPHAM. With **Twicken-ham** we are in luck: early spellings, and the place's position on a kink in the Thames, confirm that this is a *hamm* – a piece of land in a bend in a river. But now our luck runs out: we don't know whether it belonged to a man named Twicca, or was in a fork in the river. A recognisable version of the name is recorded in the early eighth century, some 1,200 years before the Rugby Football Union moved in and made Mr Twicca (if he ever existed) part of a household name.

Willesden

Most places associated with springs or streams have 'wells' in their name, but for some reason the spelling of Willesden took a different turning somewhere around the twelfth century. The –*den* comes from the same root as the ending in MORDEN and, as in Morden, is a less usual spelling than the –*don* in WIMBLEDON; but they all mean 'hill'. So Willesden is either a hill by a stream or a spring by a hill or a hill near a spring or some other combination of the two.

Neasden, in the same borough comes from the same Old English source: in this case it was a nose-shaped hill.

BARNET

Like much of North London – indeed, much of the British Isles once upon a time – Barnet used to be heavily wooded and burning was the easiest way to clear it. That's what the name tells us: this is 'land cleared by burning'. The Friern part of Friern Barnet means friars or brothers, because the Knights Hospitaller owned land here in the thirteenth century and doubtless provided accommodation for weary travellers. For more about these military orders of friars, see the box *In the Name of the Law*, page 139.

In the sixteenth century Barnet was granted a Royal Charter permitting it to hold a twice-yearly horse fair. This became famous enough to inspire a piece of rhyming slang: 'Barnet Fair' or 'barnet' is cockney for 'hair'.

Burnt Oak

We have seen elsewhere that trees were often used as boundary markers or meeting points (see FAIRLOP for a particularly fine example), and there was no reason to demote a tree just because it happened to have been struck by lightning, as is likely to have been the case here.

Cockfosters

The West Lodge Park Hotel in Cockfosters traces its ancestry back to the fifteenth century, when three lodges were built to house the foresters whose job it was to protect the royal forest of ENFIELD Chase.

Once the West Lodge ceased to be a foresters' haunt, Charles II's Secretary of State Henry Coventry (after whom COVENTRY STREET is named) lived there; John Evelyn visited in 1676 and was impressed:

> *It is a very pretty place, the house commodious, the gardens handsome, and our entertainment very free... That which I most wondered at was that, in the compass of twenty-five miles, yet within fourteen of London, there is not a house, barn, church, or building, besides three lodges. To this Lodge are three great ponds, and some few inclosures, the rest a desert, yet stored with no less than 3,000 deer. These are pretty retreats for gentlemen, especially for those who are studious and lovers of privacy.*

Why am I sharing all this with you? Well, because the name Cock-fosters tells us that it was the home of the chief foresters. *Foster* was an Elizabethan variant of *forester;* the *cock* part comes from an old meaning, 'a leader or chief man', which survives in the expression 'cock of the walk', an undisputed leader.

Colindale

When the expansion of the railways brought development to this area in the 1890s, Colindale was 'a suburban outpost near the old hamlet of Colindeep'. The earlier name, which persisted in various spellings until the nineteenth century, gives some help with the meaning: Colindale sits in a deep valley or dale, and used to be associated with a sixteenth-century family called Collin.

Cricklewood

The ending tells us that Cricklewood was once covered in woodland. No great surprise there. More appealing is the first part of the name, which indicates that the wood was an irregular shape. Sadly, the

Middle English word from which this derives seems to have vanished: it has no connection with a crick in the back of your neck, nor with crinkle-cut chips.

Finchley

'Woodland clearing where finches are seen'. This may seem hard to believe as you come off the M1 on a Sunday night and follow the crowds back into town down the Finchley Road, but it must have been true in the thirteenth century.

Golders Green

Named after a family called Golder or Goulder, who lived here in the sixteenth century, before it was standard to use apostrophes to indicate possession (see BARONS COURT and PARSONS GREEN). In 1895 Golders Green was still sufficiently far out of town for a Jewish cemetery to be established here; seven years later a (secular) crematorium was opened across the road. Neither of these things would have been countenanced in an urban district (see KENSAL GREEN for more about nineteenth-century London's concern with the disposal of the dead).

Golders Green Crematorium, although the first in London, was far from being the first in the country – that honour goes to Woking, where the Council of the Cremation Society bought land adjacent to the cemetery in the early 1880s, a year or two before cremation became legal in the UK. It promptly fell victim to an early example of nimbyism:

> *The inhabitants of Woking…showed strong antipathy to the crematorium and, led by the vicar, a small but zealous deputation appealed to the Home Secretary, Sir Richard Cross, to prohibit the use of the building.*

Sir Richard duly did prohibit it, partly on the perfectly reasonable grounds that cremation could be used to disguise a death caused by violence or poison. The Cremation Society continued its campaign, however, and in 1885 the practice was legalised. By the end of that year, Woking had performed three cremations, out of a total of almost 600,000 deaths in the UK. But fashions change and cremation is no longer as controversial as it used to be: in the century and a bit that it has been in operation, Golders Green Crematorium has performed more than 300,000 cremations, despite the fact that it is now very much in a built-up area.

Hendon

'Place on a high hill'. Go to the church of St Mary, around which the original hamlet developed, and you'll see that this is still true.

Whetstone

Oddly enough, this is almost certainly a name that can be taken at face value: it probably means that stones suitable for making whetstones (for sharpening knives and the like) were found here. They might have had the right density of grit or have been of a convenient shape – difficult to tell, as they would all have been used up long ago. There is a place in Leicestershire called Whetstone and one in Derbyshire which has simplified itself to Wheston, but both have the same derivation.

ENFIELD

The ending of this is self-explanatory; the en- may come from a personal name ('open ground associated with someone called Eana') or from an Old English word for lamb ('open ground where lambs are reared'). Whatever the meaning, it was within the large wooded area known as Enfield Chase, whose carers lived at COCKFOSTERS. 'Chase', related to the French *chasse* meaning a hunt, here means an unenclosed area of land designated for hunting or for the rearing of animals to be hunted.

Arnos Grove

'Grove' is yet another reference to woodland (see various examples throughout this chapter) and this one was associated with a family called Arnold, who lived here in the fourteenth century. If they'd been born a few hundred years later, their place could well have ended up being called Arnie's Grove, so they are probably grateful to have made their mark before that particular abbreviation came along.

HARINGEY

Believe it or not, Haringey is closely related to Hornsey and both come from the same root, meaning either 'enclosure in the grey wood' or 'enclosure belonging to a man called Haring'. The area was originally called Haringeie, later Haringay, and this gradually evolved into Hornsey. Then in the eighteenth century a wealthy local built a house which he called Harringay (with two rs), for the sort of nostalgic reasons that today inspire people to use 'Ye Olde'. Thus Harringay grew up as the neighbourhood round Harringay House, separate from but adjacent to Hornsey. Finally in 1965 the London Borough of Haringey was created, encompassing both the pre-existing districts. Confused? You may well be, but take comfort in the thought that no matter how you choose to spell Haringey, there is likely to be some historical justification for it. Even if it is H-O-R-N-S-E-Y.

Alexandra Palace

Opened in 1863, Alexandra Palace was named after the newlywed Princess of Wales, wife of the future Edward VII. Destined to be called 'the People's Palace' until the new princess came along, and still sometimes referred to by that name, it was never actually a palace; it was conceived as a recreation centre with surrounding park for the vast number of Londoners who yearned for open spaces (see Finsbury Park under FINSBURY/HIGHBURY for a similar amenity of about the same date).

Alexandra Palace opened in 1875 and attracted 120,000 visitors in just over two weeks, after which it promptly burnt down. Rebuilt within two years, it now boasted a Great Hall that became home to what was said to be the finest concert organ in Europe, driven by two steam engines and a huge set of bellows. In 1936 the first ever BBC Television transmissions were made here and the palace remained a centre of BBC-TV broadcasting for twenty years. As such it was much despised by established radio actors, who felt that television could never aspire to the artistic heights of sound broadcasting. After another fire and restoration in the 1980s, it is now primarily a concert hall and an exhibition and conference centre.

Without intending any disrespect to the late Queen Alexandra, no Londoner would ever refer to her palace by its full name: it is always 'Ally Pally', a nickname said to have been conferred by the singer Gracie Fields.

Crouch End

Have a quick look back at the box on *The Friars* (page 25) and you'll be on the right track with this name. *Crouch* comes from a medieval word for 'cross' and there must once have been a prominent cross – probably marking a crossroads – here. If you look at a modern street map, you will still see four major roads converging on Crouch End Broadway. 'End' in this instance means an outlying district, so in the fifteenth century Crouch End would have been 'the outlying district round the cross at the crossroads'. You may feel that today's version is neater.

Nearby Crouch Hill derives from the same crossroads.

Muswell Hill

The 'well' part of this derives from the natural wells or springs here, from which a conduit brought water into the City in medieval times. The first part of the name comes from the Old English for 'moss' and suggests it was a mossy or boggy spring.

Seven Sisters

Samuel Lewis's *Topographical Dictionary of England*, dated 1848, describes:

> ...*a remarkable circular clump of elm-trees called the Seven Sisters, in the centre of which was formerly a walnut-tree, that, according to tradition, never increased in size, though it continued annually to bear leaves: these trees appear to have been at their full growth in 1631, but no authentic account of their being planted is extant.*

The trees were on an area of common land called Page Green, near the current Seven Sisters station, and had given their name to the area by 1732.

Elms don't really care for London's clay soil, so even before Dutch elm disease struck most of the elms in England the sisters had had to be replanted more than once. They – or their daughters – were still around in the 1950s, but a replacement planting inaugurated by the newly formed Tree Trust for HARINGEY in 1997 took the sensible approach of choosing a tree better suited to the conditions. The circle now consists of seven hornbeams, a tree that likes the soil, is pollution-resistant and is historically appropriate: it formed part of the ancient woodland that once covered much of North London.

The suggestion that the original seven elms were planted by seven (human) sisters as they were leaving the local tavern and about to go their separate ways is surely fanciful; though if they had spent much time in the tavern it might explain why they made such an ill-considered choice of tree.

Turnpike Lane

A turnpike was originally a horizontal wooden crossbar turning on a vertical post, set up to allow pedestrians to pass but stopping horses and vehicles. It was also known as a turnstile, and lanes called Great Turnstile and Little Turnstile still exist on the south side of High HOLBORN, showing where barriers once controlled access to Lincoln's Inn Fields (see the box *In the Name of the Law*, page 139). As more roads were built and traffic increased, the turnpike became more commonly a gate, designed to stop anyone going through until they had paid a toll which in theory went towards the upkeep of the roads; in practice it more often found its way into the pocket of the local landowner. The turnpike after which Turnpike Lane is named stood at the junction of two main roads, near the present station.

WALTHAM FOREST

Etymologically Waltham Forest and Walthamstow are completely different, but they have morphed into each other over the years. Waltham means 'forest estate' and Waltham Forest was an early name for part of Epping Forest (see FOREST GATE). Walthamstow used to be Wilcumestou, which probably meant 'a (holy) place where guests are welcome'. But confusion brought about by its proximity to Waltham Forest led to its being called Walthamstowe as early as the fifteenth century.

To bring the story up to date, Waltham Forest no longer exists as a forest but the London Borough of Waltham Forest was created in 1965 and Walthamstow is part of it.

Wanstead

The *–stead* part here is simple enough: as in HAMPSTEAD, it means a place. The beginning is less certain: it may be related to the modern *wen*, 'a lump or tumour' or to *wain*, as in haywain, 'a wagon'. So Wanstead may be 'place by the lumpy hill' or 'place associated with wagons'. In this flat area it is tempting to plump for the latter, but there is no real evidence either way.

NEWHAM

Unlike Newgate (see the box *The City Gates*, page 37) and many other places that call themselves 'new' long after this has ceased to be accurate, the London Borough of Newham is genuinely new – at least by the standard of most names in this book. It was created in 1965 and combined the older boroughs of East and West Ham. The *ham* in this instance is not the usual 'homestead' of Streatham nor even the 'land in the bend of the river' of Fulham; it comes from another meaning of *hamm*, 'low-lying land enclosed by marsh'. A place called Hamme is recorded here before the Domesday Book and the first mentions of East and West Ham are found by the thirteenth century.

Canning Town

This name was created for an industrial development that grew up near the Royal Victoria Dock in the mid-nineteenth century. No one is certain whom it commemorates, although it is almost certainly not the Prime Minister George Canning, who had been dead for twenty years by then. A 1973 guide to Essex says firmly that it is a name of unknown origin, but others speculate. It may have been the Prime Minister's son, Charles, First Earl Canning (1812–62), but this seems odd: he was a peer without portfolio at the time, having recently been First Commissioner of Woods and Forests, with no obvious connection to the East End. Samuel Canning is an equally unlikely offering – he became a distinguished engineer but was only twenty-eight years old at the date in question. Or another engineer, also George Canning. The only thing we can be sure of is that Canning Town was originally concerned with shipbuilding and iron works – any connection to the canning industry is purely coincidental.

Forest Gate

It may not seem very woody nowadays, but this was once the southernmost point of Epping Forest. 'Forest' in medieval speak meant 'land reserved for royal hunting'; it wasn't necessarily woodland, and the local people had the right to forage for food and fuel and to graze their livestock there. So putting up a gate to stop livestock straying out of the forest and on to the road was a sensible precaution – particularly as, at one time, Epping butter fetched the highest prices in London, making cows a valuable resource. (The area was also famous for its pork and sausages, so presumably the locals kept a close eye on their pigs, too.) The gate was there for at least 200 years before being taken down in 1883.

Silvertown

Nothing to do with silver any more than CANNING TOWN is to do with canning, although the two areas developed around the same time. S W Silver & Co was a rubber manufacturer that opened a factory near Ham Creek in 1852 and gave its name to the surrounding area.

Stratford

This has the same derivation at Stratford-upon-Avon and means a ford by a (probably Roman) road. The Old English *stræt* derives from the Latin *via strata*, 'paved road', and this road ran from London to Colchester, one of the most important towns in Roman Britain. The river Lea (see LEYTON/LEYTONSTONE) meanders about all over the place in the East End and a ford by which to cross it would have been an important feature of the landscape and a good reason for a settlement to develop.

REDBRIDGE

There used to be a red bridge here, crossing the river Roding; it was taken down in 1922 to make way for what is now part of the A12. The tube station, on what is rather tongue-twistingly called the FAIRLOP

Loop of the Central Line, opened as late as 1947, providing further evidence of the phenomenon that a place name will linger on long after the reason for it has vanished.

BARKING AND DAGENHAM

Like NEWHAM, this is a borough formed in 1965 from the fusion of two older entities: the former founded by the followers of a man called something like Berica, and nothing to do with either dogs or insanity; the latter the home of a man called Daecca, nothing to do with the record label.

Fairlop

Perhaps surprisingly, this name does indeed come from *fair* and *lop*. An annual fair was held under the shade of a vast but lopped (pruned) oak tree. Daniel Lysons, writing in the 1790s, describes…

> …*a remarkable tree, well known by the name of Fairlop Oak. The stem, which is rough and sluted, measures, at three feet [90 cm] from the ground, about thirty-six feet [11 metres] in girth. The boughs extend about 300 feet [91 metres] in circumference. Under their shade is held a fair on the first Friday in July. It is said to have originated from a man of singular character going there annually to dine with his friends. The tree is now fenced round with a close paling about five feet [1.6 metres] high, and Mr. Forsyth's composition has been applied to its decayed branches to preserve it as much as possible from future injury.*

Sluted must be a misprint, as the only meanings the OED gives for *slute* are 'to render sluttish', which was obsolete by Lysons' time, and 'to act as a drudge or a woman of loose morals', which isn't recorded until some thirty years later and makes little sense in the context. Maybe the tree was *fluted*. William Forsyth (1737–1804) was a Scottish arboriculturalist whose pioneering 'composition' for treating injury or disease in trees contained cow dung, 'lime-rubbish of old buildings' (preferably from the ceiling), wood ash and river sand, all of which needed to be 'worked well together with a spade, and afterwards with a wooden beater, until the stuff is very smooth, like fine plaster used for the ceilings of rooms'. Those in the know were very impressed by this and named the forsythia after him.

Anyway, back to the Fairlop Oak. The tree, despite Mr Forsyth's composition, blew down in 1820, but part of it was salvaged to make a pulpit and reading desk for St Pancras Church. The desk has disappeared, but you can still drop in and admire the pulpit.

The forest in which the Fairlop Oak stood, perhaps for 1,000 years, was Hainault, part of the ancient WALTHAM FOREST. Hainault does not refer to the place in modern Belgium from which Edward III's queen, Philippa of Hainault, came. Instead it comes from the Old English for 'wood belonging to a household', in this case the monastic household of BARKING Abbey. The modern spelling does, however, come from a confusion with Queen Philippa – left to evolve logically, it would have been something more like Hineholt.

So, rather poignantly, we have here two unusual place names, both with interesting provenances, that are now known almost entirely because they are adjacent stations on a loop line of the London Underground system.

HAVERING

This is one of the many *-ing* names (see PADDINGTON, KENSINGTON, BARKING etc.) that indicate an association with an otherwise unknown Anglo-Saxon chieftain. In the Middle Ages the place was known as Havering-atte-Bower, *bower* being a variant on *bury*, meaning a manor. In the case of Havering it was a royal retreat, established as a hunting lodge by Edward the Confessor (1042–66) and expanded and used by a number of monarchs until Stuart times.

Upminster

A minster was originally a large church in which monks generally lived apart from the wider world but offered hospitality to travellers and 'ministered' to the sick. In the seventh century the Holy Island of Lindisfarne sent a monk down to this part of the world to found a minster, and although it disappeared long ago the modern church of St Laurence stands on the same site. The 'up' part of the name simply means that the minster stood on high ground.

OUTLYING BOROUGHS
SOUTH OF THE RIVER

A shorter chapter than the previous one, for two reasons. One, there are appreciably fewer boroughs south of the river; and two, the south-east was, at the time the London Underground was developing, well served by the railways. As a result, fewer of its names have become familiar to those who stand on tube platforms waiting despairingly for the next train to UPMINSTER or UXBRIDGE.

It remains an intriguing area, however, once far enough from town for the scandalous to live in discreet retirement. Like the outlying areas of the previous chapter, it has long since been subsumed into the urban sprawl, though it still has a full complement of green spaces, including the two largest Royal Parks.

RICHMOND

Anyone familiar with Shakespeare's *Richard III* will know that Henry VII was Earl of Richmond before he came king. That was Richmond in Yorkshire, whose name is Old French for 'strong hill'. Around 1500, when Henry was well established on the throne, he built himself a new palace by the Thames, named it after his previous title and decreed that the surrounding area, previously known as West Sheen, should henceforward also be called Richmond. Sheen, from the Old English for 'sheds or shelters', is recorded as early as the tenth century and it is not clear why; we know that there was a palace here in the fourteenth century and a Carthusian monastery in the fifteenth but, however hospitable they may have been, they are both far too late to have been the original shelters.

Some 500 years after West Sheen ceased to trouble cartographers, East Sheen and North Sheen are still on the map. There seems never to have been a South Sheen, probably because the names of West, East and North Sheen indicated that they were to the west, east and north of the original manor. To the south was what is now Richmond Park, enclosed as a royal hunting ground by Charles I in the 1630s. The enclosure was an unpopular move. Some of the land was in private hands when Charles declared his intentions and the owners were unwilling to give it up. The king didn't care: one report tells us that 'he did in fact begin building the surrounding wall before he had obtained the consent of his subjects, and thereby caused a great deal of bitterness'. This was the man who ended up being beheaded, remember: he was severely lacking in diplomacy when it came to dealing with his subjects.

Barnes

A straightforward name: this was originally a place near a barn or barns. Barnes does boast an intriguingly named street, however. Castelnau was the creation of the Boileau family, who lived in nearby MORT-LAKE and developed this area in the 1820s–1840s. Their ancestral home was in the south of France, at Castelnau de la Garde, near Nîmes.

Bushy

The name probably means 'bushy' and Bushy Park, the second largest (after RICHMOND) of the Royal Parks, was a park with bushes. Originally – like many of London's large open spaces – a royal hunting ground, it became a formal park in the seventeenth century. Less bushy than it used to be, it still has an abundance of trees, notably the famous Chestnut Avenue designed by Christopher Wren.

Ham

Like FULHAM, this comes from *hamm*, 'a place in the bend of the river', as a look at a map of the area will explain: the Thames is in one of its more sinuous moods at this point.

Kew

The modern name is a confusingly abbreviated form of Cayho, which is how it was recorded in the fourteenth century. That old ending tells us that it was a projecting piece of land. The beginning is less clear: it may mean that Kew was an important landing place, in which case it is connected to *quay*; or it may be *key*-shaped and linked to that modern word.

Mortlake

A place called Mortlake that has a big cemetery sounds as if it ought to be to do with death. But this is nothing more than a macabre coincidence: the *mort* here refers to a salmon in its third year. The word – unfamiliar in standard English but still in use in some regional vocabularies – dates back to the Domesday Book, which records a recognisable form of Mortlake and mentions a fishery that had once been the property of Earl Harold (he who lost his life at the Battle of Hastings in 1066).

KINGSTON

This name is found all over England and means 'the king's manor or estate'. But the one in South London is the oldest Kingston in the country and the Royal Borough of Kingston upon Thames is the oldest royal borough. Alfred the Great's son, known as Edward the Elder, was crowned here in 900, and the place has been deemed to have royal connections ever since.

MERTON

Turn *Mer-* into the modern 'mere' and you have it: 'farmstead or estate by a pool'. The pool formed part of the river Wandle (see WANDSWORTH) and Merton grew and prospered because of its share in the mill-based industries mentioned in that entry. At the beginning of the nineteenth century it was far enough out of town to suit people who wanted to live 'retired from the world'. Three of its most famous inhabitants were Lord Nelson, his mistress Lady Hamilton and the lady's husband, who lived here for several years from 1801 in one of history's more bizarre *ménages à trois*. The household included an illegitimate daughter, named Horatia after her father, which makes a bit of a nonsense of the adults' professed desire for discretion – did they not think that even in this secluded spot people would ask the name of the little girl and put two and two together? Nor are they forgotten 200 years later: if you come out of South Wimbledon tube and stroll along Merton High Street you will pass, in quick succession, Hamilton, Hardy, Nelson and Victory Roads, commemorating respectively Nelson's mistress, his flag captain (of 'Kiss me, Hardy' legend), the man himself and his flagship.

Colliers Wood

Not associated with coal mining, but derived from the same source: the cottage industry here was charcoal burning, which produced what was in medieval times an important fuel.

Morden

As with MERTON, you need to tinker with this: then you get *moor down*, which translates as 'hill above marshy ground'.

Wimbledon

The *–don* ending here is the more usual spelling of the *–den* in MORDEN and means a hill. The first part derives from an Old English personal name and in the tenth century the combination produced the rather unwieldy Wunemannedune. That plethora of *n*s would have been a real tongue-twister and the changing of one 'liquid' consonant (*l, m, n* or *r*) for another is a common feature of the 'if it's hard to pronounce, change it' school of place-name development. Thus Wimeldon, introducing an *l*, had emerged by the early thirteenth century. The appearance of a *b* in the middle is what the experts call inorganic and you and I might call random, but soon led to Wimbeldon and thence to the modern spelling.

SUTTON

One of the commonest of English place names, this means 'southern farmstead or village'. So either there was a Norton and a Middleton round about, or it lay to the south of a larger or more established settlement.

CROYDON

From the earliest times saffron was valued as a medicinal plant, as a dye and as a food flavouring. It is related to the crocus, hence its Old English name of *crog*. In Croydon the *-don* ending means not hill as in Wimbledon but dene or valley. Thus Croydon, before it became... well, the place it is now... was a valley where wild saffron grew.

BROMLEY

'Clearing or glade where broom grows'. The name is recorded as early as 862, when Ethelbert, King of Kent, granted land to the Bishops of Rochester to form a manor here. The bishops held on to it until 1845 – a remarkable achievement given the changing attitudes to the church and to land ownership that had come and gone during the intervening millennium.

Chislehurst

The ending *–hurst* generally means a wooded hill and the first part of Chislehurst indicates that it was gravelly – it's the same derivation as the famously stony Chesil Beach.

Penge

One of the oldest names in this book, Penge comes from the Celtic language that was spoken in Britain before the Anglo-Saxon invasion. *Pen* derives from the Celtic word for hill and is still found in place names where Old English never really ousted the ancient tongue: Penzance in Cornwall, Pen-y-Ghent in Yorkshire, Pen y fan and other peaks in Wales. The ending means 'wood' (it's a corruption of *coed*, which also survives in many Welsh names), so Penge was situated at the top of the wood.

Why it should have come down to us as Penge rather than, say, Upwood, is a matter for speculation: perhaps a Celtic-speaking community hung on here after the Saxons took over London.

BEXLEY

Exactly the same as BROMLEY, except that a different sort of vegetation was found here: this is the clearing where box grew. Box also grew on Box Hill in Surrey and in various places called Boxgrove and Boxford, so why the vowel should have changed here but not there is another matter for conjecture, but it is recorded as Bex- by the fourteenth century.

Sidcup

Cup here is related to *copp*, a less common Old English word for a hill (most of them ended up as some variation of *–don*, as in WIMBLEDON). It's impossible to be 100 per cent sure about the beginning, but it probably indicates a seat-shaped or flat-topped hill. A *Topographical Dictionary of England* dated 1848 describes Sidcup as a hamlet and tells us that there are several gentlemen's seats in the neighbourhood, but that probably isn't entirely relevant to the seat shape of the derivation.

BIBLIOGRAPHY

Ackroyd, Peter *London: the biography* (Chatto & Windus, 2000)

Baker, T F T, and R B Pugh (editors), *A History of the County of Middlesex* (Victoria County History,1976)

Besant, Sir Walter, *The Fascination of London: The Thames* (A & C Black, 1903)

Billings, Malcolm *London: a companion to its history and archaeology* (Kyle Cathie, 1994)

Dowsing, James *Guide to Pimlico* (Sunrise Press, 1981)

Flavell, Linda and Roger *Dictionary of Word Origins* (new edition, Kyle Cathie, 2010)

Gardiner, Juliet, and Neil Wenborn (editors) *The History Today Companion to British History* (Collins & Brown, 1995)

Hibbert, Christopher *London: the biography of a city* (Longmans, 1969)

Lysons, Daniel *The Environs of London* (1792–6); online at www.british-history.ac.uk

Mills, A D *A Dictionary of London Place Names* (2nd edition, Oxford University Press, 2010)

Renier, Hannah *Lambeth Past* (Historical Publications, 2006)

Richardson, John *Covent Garden Past* (Historical Publications, 1995)

Rogerson, Barnaby *London: A Collection of Poetry of Place* (2nd edition, Eland, 2010)

Stapleton, Alan *London Alleys, Byways and Courts* (John Lane The Bodley Head, 1924)

Stow, John, with introduction and notes by Charles Lethbridge Kingsford *A Survey of London* (Oxford University Press, 1908, revised 1971: Kingsford's text, based on the 1603 edition and regarded as the standard version, is also available online at www.british-history.ac.uk)

Strype, John *A Survey of the Cities of London and Westminster* (1720; online at www.hrionline.ac.uk/strype/index.jsp)

Trench, Richard & Ellis Hillman *London Under London* (John Murray, 1985)

Walford, Edward *Old and New London* (Cassell, Petter & Galpin,1878; online at www.british-history.ac.uk)

Weinreb, Ben & Christopher Hibbert (eds) *The London Encyclopaedia* (revised edition, Macmillan, 1993)

Wheatley, H B *London Past and Present* (John Murray, 1891)

In addition the following websites were particularly useful:

www.coventgarden.uk.com for the history of Bedfordbury

www.homecountiespubs.co.uk/chobham/history/ for Richard II and white harts

www.lsm.org.uk/about/bounds.html for beating the bounds at Gospel Oak

INDEX